DISCOVERING SCIENCE   ON
YOUR
OWN

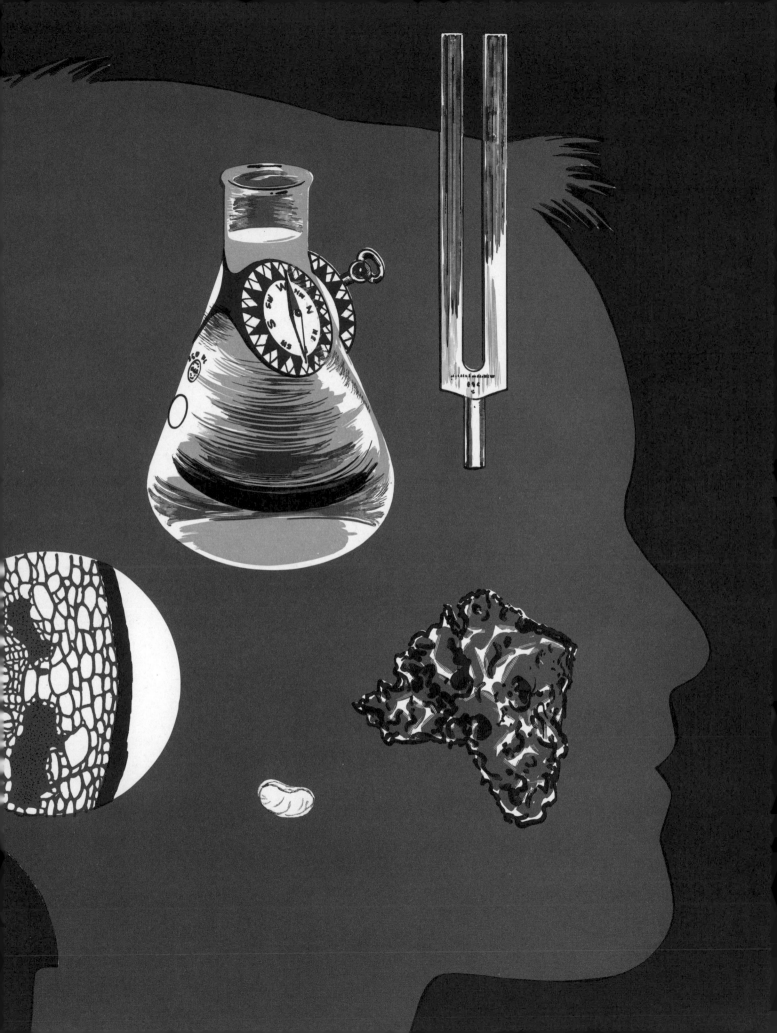

DIS·COVER·ING

BY ILLA PODENDORF   ARTIST: ROBERT BORJA

SCIENCE

ON YOUR OWN

GROSSET & DUNLAP · Publishers · NEW YORK

A CHILDRENS PRESS BOOK

Anyone who visits Illa Podendorf's classroom at the Laboratory School, University of Chicago, is soon aware that her successful teaching is based on encouraging children to work on their own and to investigate and solve problems as scientists do.

Discovery through experiments and activities is fun. But children also learn more by developing their own concepts through first hand experiences. They improve their skills of observing, collecting information and thinking. And as they do experiments, children improve their reading skill and the capacity to follow directions intelligently. Knowledge gained through personal discovery is knowledge retained to build upon.

There are many experiences in discovering science in this book through which children see or hear or otherwise observe what happens in a very small part of the universe. In this way they build understandings and concepts that help explain events in a larger universe—the goal of all scientists.

Paul E. Blackwood
Specialist for Elementary Science
Office of Education
U.S. Department of Health,
Education and Welfare

LIBRARY OF CONGRESS CATALOG CARD NUMBER: 6211408
COPYRIGHT, 1962, CHILDRENS PRESS, PRINTED IN THE U.S.A.

CONTENTS

SCIENCE

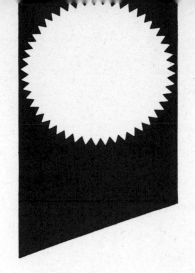

Almost everyone has an idea about what science is. I am sure, however, if you were to ask different people what they think science is they all would not give you the same answer. Some might say it is a subject which we study in school, or it is facts about the world in which we live. Still others might say it is a way (method) to find out more about our environment. All of these answers would be correct — science is all of these things.

There is a great deal known about the world in which we live and particularly about our immediate environment. Some of the things which are known were discovered quite by accident, others were the results of carefully planned experiments or investigations.

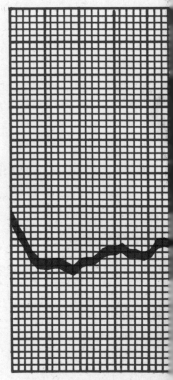

DISCOVERIES

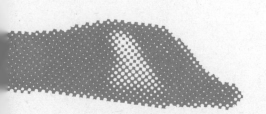

Almost every day new discoveries are being made about the inside of the earth, about things on the earth, and about things far out in space.

When one scientist or group of scientists discovers something new, this new discovery may become a part of the basis upon which other scientists make more discoveries. It would be very unnecessary for a scientist to discover over again something which is already known before going on to try for new discoveries. It is important that accurate records be kept of all new findings and new ideas. It is also important that scientists study carefully and understand what is known about a particular subject or about old discoveries. All this is more true now than it once was. When the Wright brothers invented the airplane they had to get most of the ideas themselves because there was so little known about how to make an airplane that would fly. Now the work, ideas and cooperation of many scientists and mathematicians are necessary to make space travel possible.

Many boys and girls like to discover for themselves some things about science. To discover for ourselves is an exciting way to learn some of the things which are known to scientists and to better understand what we see going on around us.

This book contains suggestions for making some discoveries which may be new to the persons making them although they may be known to scientists. Some of these suggestions are experiments, while others are not. In each experiment there is a question and a suggestion for finding the answer. Something happens in an experiment. This usually helps to give the answer to the question. Although some of the suggestions are not really experiments they, too, are fun and will help boys and girls to better understand their environment and the world in which they live.

Illa Podendorf

13

THE

TO KNOW MORE ABOUT THE EARTH PEOPLE STUDY GEOLOGY.
GEOLOGY IS A STUDY ABOUT THE EARTH, AND THE ROCKS AND MINERALS
OF WHICH IT IS MADE. GEOLOGISTS TRY TO FIND OUT HOW THE EARTH
WAS FORMED, WHAT IT IS ON THE INSIDE, AND HOW IT IS CHANGING
ON THE OUTSIDE. IN THIS SECTION OF THE BOOK THERE ARE THINGS
TO DO WHICH WILL HELP YOU TO DISCOVER FOR YOURSELF INTERESTING
FACTS ABOUT THE EARTH.

EARTH

DOES WATER MOVE BETTER THROUGH SOME SOIL THAN THROUGH OTHER SOIL?

If you have a piece of blotting paper about three inches long and an inch wide and also a piece of file card the same size you could use them to help find an answer to the question. Measure one-half inch from the end of each of the pieces of paper. Draw a line across on each of them. Now get a bowl of water. Hold the two pieces of paper so that they do not touch each other, but are close together. Put them in the bowl of water so that the pencil line is at the top of the water with one-half inch of each paper under water. Watch carefully. What did you notice? You are almost sure to have noticed that the water went faster and farther in the blotting paper — it is not pressed so hard as the paper in the file card. You may wish to do this over again to see whether the same thing happens. Now you have discovered for yourself why water goes through some soil more easily than through other soil.

CAN YOU PREDICT ACCURATELY WHAT WILL HAPPEN IN THIS EXPERIMENT?

Put a teaspoonful of granulated sugar in a little pile on a plate. Put a teaspoonful of powdered sugar on the same plate but about one-fourth inch away from the other sugar. Make a little pile of the powdered sugar, too. Now get ready to put a few drops of water which has been colored with some cake coloring in between the two piles of sugar. Before you do it decide which pile of sugar you think will get wet first. This is your prediction. Now do the experiment and find out whether or not your prediction was right. If you remember the experiment with the blotter and the card — you probably made a correct prediction.

The granulated sugar got wet first. It got wet first because it was not packed so hard.

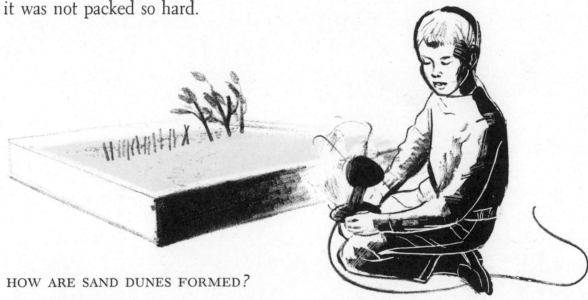

HOW ARE SAND DUNES FORMED?

Sand dunes are formed by the wind. You can see how it happens by spreading some sand evenly over the bottom of a sand box. Connect up a small electric fan so that it blows over the surface of the sand. Move the position of the fan from time to time to see what happens. You might spread the sand evenly again and place in it some twigs to look like shrubs and bushes. You might also build a fence out of toothpicks. Now turn on the fan again. You will see that wind piles sand into queer shapes and also moves piles of sand from one place to another. You may notice, too, that the fence and shrubs help a little to keep the sand from blowing away. When sand and earth are blown away it is called "wind erosion."

17

DO PLANTS HELP TO PREVENT SOIL FROM WEARING AWAY?

Use two shoe boxes of about the same size. Line each of them with aluminum foil. Fill each of them about two-thirds full of soil and in one of the boxes plant grass seeds. Water the soil in each box and set them in a suitable place for the seeds to germinate and grow.

When the grass is at least one-half inch high remove one of the ends of each box without disturbing the soil. Set the boxes side by side, on a tray or in a larger box, so that the closed ends of the boxes are about two inches higher than the open ends. This then resembles hillsides.

With a nail make three or four small holes in the bottom of a tin can. Hold the can over the closed end of one of the boxes and fill the can with water. The water will run down onto the soil like rain. Repeat this, putting the same amount of water in the tin can but hold it over the other box.

Notice what happens. Did the water run into the ground or down the hill? Did the same thing happen in each box? Did the plants in the one box help hold the water back? If there are no plants, water is much more certain to run off and carry soil with it.

Water the boxes of dirt several times the same way. Did the same thing happen? Did the erosion slow down or did it continue? Which hill will be worn down first? You are almost sure to say that the hill with no plants on it would wear away first. The washing away of soil is called "water erosion."

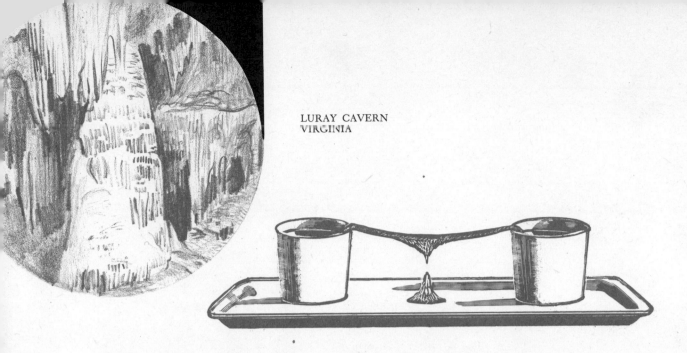

HOW DO STALACTITES AND STALAGMITES FORM?

Almost every one has visited a cave such as the one which you see in the picture. Almost every one has wondered about how the stalactites and the stalagmites were formed. If you follow the plan described on this page you may get some ideas which will help you to better understand the answer to this question.

Into a cup of water stir one-half cup of Epsom salts. After all of the Epsom salts are dissolved, pour one-half of the solution into one paper cup and the other half into another paper cup. Set the two cups about four or five inches apart on a tray. Put one end of a heavy cord or strip of cloth twisted until it is ropelike into one of the cups. Put the other end into the other cup. You may need to tape them to the cups to keep them in place properly. The heavy cord or twisted cloth should loop down a bit between the two cups. Watch what happens.

You will probably notice that the liquid drips from the string or cloth loop which is between the cups. The drip should be very slow — if it drips fast, raise the loop a bit. If you watch this long enough you may see stalactites begin to form on the loop. There might also be a little mound of Epsom salts on the tray under the string. This is a beginning of a stalagmite. The stalagmites and stalactites are formed in a cave in the same way. The only difference is they form from limewater instead of Epsom salts water.

19

WAIKITE GEYSER
NEW ZEALAND

WHAT ARE GEYSERS?

A spring of hot water and steam spurting out of the earth is a geyser. It helps to understand what causes them if you do the demonstration which is pictured on this page. Find a large beaker and a pyrex funnel which will fit into it. A kitchen pan and funnel will do but it is easier to see what happens if pyrex is used. Turn the funnel stem end up in the beaker. Place a layer of pebbles in the beaker under the funnel so that water can get under it. Fill the beaker with water about halfway up to the stem of the funnel. Place the beaker over heat and allow the water to come to a boil.

Bubbles of steam will form near the bottom of the beaker and under the funnel. The bubbles will start to rise and push water out of the stem ahead of them. This is an eruption. More bubbles will come and more pressure will be formed and soon there will be another eruption. This is a little like what happens inside the earth. In a real geyser the water is heated far down in the earth and is forced to the surface through a crooked, irregular passage way.

20

ARE ALL ROCKS THE SAME — ONE KIND JUST AS HARD AS ANOTHER KIND?

You may do this experiment to find the answer to the question. Collect together several rocks of different kinds. Try to scratch each rock with the point of a sharp knife. You will find that you can scratch some of them deeply and some of them only slightly, while others show no scratches at all. Not all rocks are the same hardness. Talc is the softest kind of rock. You can scratch it with your fingernail. Quartz is a very hard rock. You probably won't be able to scratch it with the very sharpest knife. Scientists use the hardness quality to help them identify rocks.

HOW ARE PEBBLES MADE?

Find a rock and with a hammer break it up into small pieces about the size of marbles. You will notice that each of the pieces has sharp edges. Place the small pieces in a quart fruit jar and pour water over it. The jar should be about half full. Shake the jar so that the rocks will be washed and rubbed against each other. Let the jar set for a while and shake it again. Do this several times. Now examine the rocks. Do they look the same as they did before? You will notice that the sharp edges are no longer so sharp. Some of the rocks may be worn off so that they are quite round. If the rocks are a soft kind of rock like talc they will wear smooth quickly. If it is a hard rock like quartz it will take a long time to wear smooth.

21

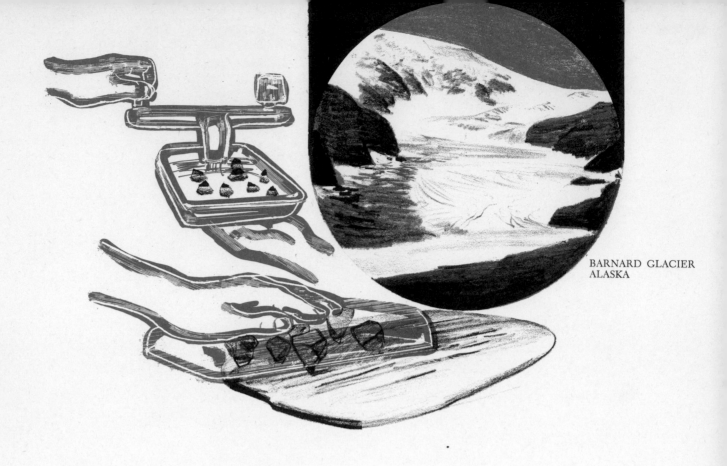

BARNARD GLACIER
ALASKA

HOW HAVE GLACIERS BEEN ABLE TO SCRATCH ROCKS?

Discover for yourself how the scratches are made on rocks. Follow this plan. Find a dozen or more rocks which are not yet worn smooth, but instead have sharp edges. They should be no bigger than a small marble. Put them in an ice tray and fill the tray with water. Put it in the freezer to freeze solid. After it is frozen, spread some plasticine or clay more or less evenly over a smooth surface. You might use more than one color of clay and make it look as though there are rocks and boulders in the soil. Take the ice with the stones in it from the tray. As soon as the ice begins to melt, place it on top of the clay. Pretend that the ice is a glacier and that the glacier is moving over the boulders and rocks and soil under it. Press on it gently and move it across the clay. You will notice that the rough stones leave scratches on the clay which represents the soil, boulders, and rocks of the earth. If this were a real glacier it would leave scratches on the rocks or boulders under it, as its weight caused it to move downward.

22

HOW ARE CRYSTALS FORMED?

Discover for yourself something about how crystals are formed. Stir some **Epsom** salts into water. Use about 4 tablespoonfuls of water and two of **Epsom** salts. When the salts are dissolved pour a bit of the solution in a large flat tray and let it stand in open air. The liquid should almost cover the bottom of the tray but it should not be very deep. Set the tray aside. Look at the tray each day. What do you see? After the water has evaporated there are crystals left. The crystal are crystals of epsom salts. Do they form beautiful patterns much like frost?

HOW DO CRYSTALS GROW?

Find three or four lumps of soft coal or of charcoal which are about the size of a tennis ball. Place them in a dish which is not very deep. Now pour four tablespoonfuls of water in a cup. Stir four tablespoonfuls of salt which is not iodized into the water and add four tablespoonfuls of liquid bluing to it. Now add one tablespoonful of household ammonia. Pour this mixture over the lumps of coal or charcoal. If you want it to have more color, add a few drops of vegetable coloring here and there over the coal. Set the dish in a safe place and watch to see what happens. The crystals will grow larger and larger. Crystals do not grow as plants and animals grow. Plants and animals grow from the inside. Crystals get bigger by adding layers and layers on the outside.

CRYSTAL
FORMS

23

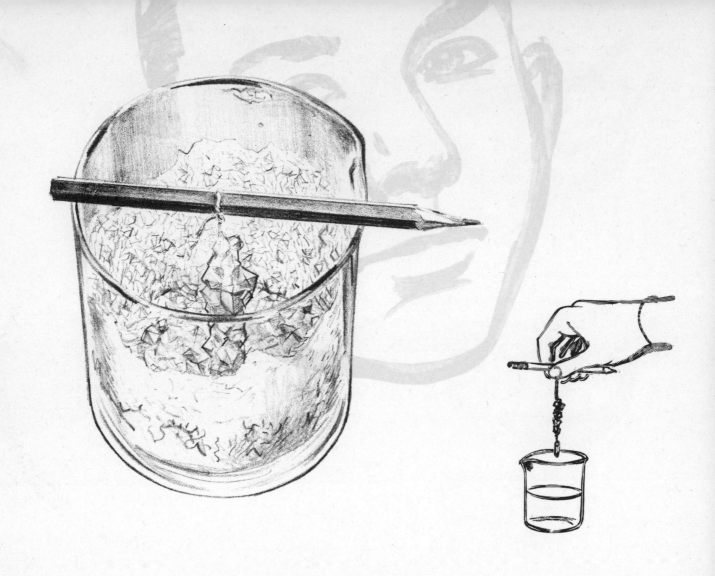

WHAT IS ANOTHER WAY IN WHICH CRYSTALS ARE MADE?

Put a cupful of water into a pan or beaker and heat it until it begins to boil. Remove it from the heat and add powdered alum until no more will dissolve in the liquid. Now tie one end of a string to a stick. Tie a paper clip on the other end of the string. Lay the stick across the top of the pan or beaker and let the string hang down into the solution. The paper clip will weight down the string. Set the solution aside in a safe place to cool. It should cool very slowly. Crystals of alum are almost sure to form on the string. Crystals in rocks are sometimes formed much like the alum crystals were formed. The slower the liquid cools the larger the crystals are likely to be.

24

HOW ARE FOSSIL CASTS MADE?

Use a small plastic bowl. Put some plasticine clay in the bowl and work it down firmly so that it is very smooth on top. Find a couple of shells which will fit nicely on the clay. Place them on the clay and press them down in the clay firmly. When they are removed a nice print is left. Now mix plaster of Paris and water so that you have a thin paste. Pour the plaster of Paris into the mold or prints of shells. After four or five hours the plaster of Paris is hard enough for you to take it out of the mold. When you have taken it out you have a cast of the shells. This is one kind of fossil.

Real fossil casts are made in much the same way. Prints made in thick mud become filled in with limewater. The water evaporates out and, after thousands of years there is a limestone cast.

25

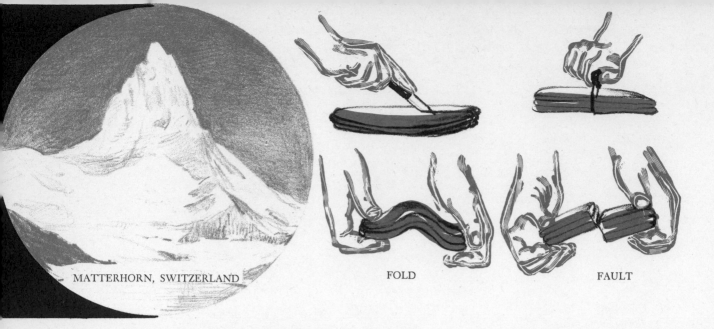

MATTERHORN, SWITZERLAND

FOLD

FAULT

HOW ARE SOME MOUNTAINS FORMED?

Discover for yourself how mountains are sometimes formed.

Get three or four different colors of plasticine clay. Pat an equal-sized piece of each color down flat on a smooth surface so that it is about one half-inch thick.

Now stack the pieces of clay on top of one another, and press them down together. There will be a thinner layer of each color now. Use a sharp knife and cut down through the center so that you have two parts or stacks. You may use the knife and trim the edges of the stacks if you wish.

Now place one of your hands on each side of one of the stacks and push your hands together. The clay will fold up in the center as you see in the picture. Sometimes layers of the earth are pushed up into a fold by pressure from within the earth, and form mountains. This is called a folded mountain.

Now with the other stack of clay you can discover another way in which mountains are made. With the knife, cut down through the layers of clay. Keep the two cut sides touching each other but raise one of them above the other so that the layers do not match. Mountains are formed in this way when a crack comes in the layers of rock, as it sometimes does, and a great force from inside the earth pushes one side up above the other. This is called a faulted mountain. Folded and faulted mountains are found on many parts of the earth.

26

MT. VESUVIUS, ITALY

HOW IS A VOLCANIC MOUNTAIN FORMED?

Use a tray or piece of metal at least a foot square. Set an empty
tin can which is about six inches tall in the middle of the tray or metal.
Mix some plaster of Paris into a thin paste and put a piece of cloth which
is about a yard square into it. When the cloth is wet and heavy with the
plaster of Paris in it drape it around the can, arranging it in a cone
shape. Let it dry. Mix more of the plaster of Paris into a thick paste.
Pour it around the center of the top so that it will run down on the
outside as if it were molten rock. Repeat this several times — each
time being sure that your make-believe volcano is dry when more
plaster of Paris is put on it.

When you have the volcano the shape of the one in the picture
you can fit a little pan or dish into the top of it to represent the
crater. Then you may wish to paint your volcano. Red can represent
the flow of hot rock from the crater and also from the side eruptions.
Of course in a real volcano — the hot molten rock comes from the
inside of the earth. Some mountains are caused by volcanoes.

27

OBSIDIAN

PUMICE

VOLCANIC TUFF

HOW DO ROCKS FROM A VOLCANO DIFFER?

Find for yourself a piece of pumice, obsidian, volcanic tuff, basalt and granite. Drop all of them in water. What do you notice? You probably noticed air bubbles coming out of the pumice and volcanic tuff. The pumice might even float. The other three rocks went to the bottom and gave up almost no bubbles.

Now remove all of them from the water and hold a reading glass over each of them. What do you notice? You probably see many tiny spaces in the pumice and some spaces in the volcanic tuff. You will notice the smooth shiny surface of the obsidian. You will notice, too, the crystals in the granite and basalt. These and many other kinds of rocks are made from volcanic action. Rocks such as pumice and volcanic tuff come from explosive-like volcanoes. The pumice is hardened foam and volcanic tuff is cinder-like. Other kinds of volcanoes are not so explosive. The hot melted rock, from down in the earth, is pushed to the top and some of it spills over. The obsidian cools so very fast as it comes out of the volcano that there are no crystals and it looks like shiny glass. Some of the melted material cools and hardens into rock while it is still inside the earth. The slower it cools the larger are the crystals of which the rock is made. Granite and basalt are made this way. If you look at the basalt and granite carefully you will decide that the granite cooled more slowly than the basalt. The crystals in it are larger.

28

MONUMENT VALLEY
ARIZONA

NOW
YOU
KNOW
THAT:

The study of the history of the earth
and how it is formed is called Geology.

Water moves more easily through some
things than through others.

Sand and earth are blown about by
wind. This is wind erosion.

Soil may be washed away by water.
This is called water erosion.

Plants help prevent wind and water
erosion.

Stalagmites and stalactites form
from minerals in dripping water.

Steam from water heated within the
earth causes a geyser.

Not all rocks are the same hardness.

Small, sharp pieces of rock worn
smooth become pebbles.

The slower the melted material from
inside the earth cools, the larger
are the crystals of which rock is made.

A fossil cast is made over thousands
of years as lime in water hardens in
a print in the mud.

Mountains are sometimes formed by
great pressure from within the earth.

Mountains may be made by folding,
faulting, or volcanic action.

29

ASTRONOMY IS THE STUDY OF THE SUN, MOON, STARS, PLANETS AND OTHER BODIES IN THE UNIVERSE. SCIENTISTS WHO STUDY ASTRONOMY STUDY THE MOTIONS, DISTANCES, SIZES AND ALSO WHAT THESE BODIES IN THE SKY ARE MADE OF AS WELL AS HOW THEY MIGHT HAVE BEEN FORMED. THEY ARE PARTICULARLY INTERESTED IN HOW EACH OF THE BODIES AFFECT EACH OTHER AS THEY MOVE IN THE SKY. HERE ARE SOME THINGS TO DO WHICH MAY HELP YOU TO DISCOVER FOR YOURSELF SOME THINGS ABOUT THE SKY AND WHAT IS IN IT.

ASTRONOMY

HOW CAN WE SEE THE SUN?

Everyone knows that it is dangerous to try to look directly at the sun without something to shut out some of the very bright light. Scientists do not look at the sun through a telescope unless there is something to protect their eyes from the light. You can get a better look at the sun by using a smoked glass. Find an ordinary piece of glass and hold it over a burning candle or any other smoking flame until it is covered with soot. Now hold the glass between you and the sun. The soot will shut out part of the sun's light and this makes it possible for you to have a more careful view. It is wise to use a piece of smoked glass to view an eclipse of the sun. Even in an eclipse the sunlight is so bright it is hard for you to see the eclipse well.

32

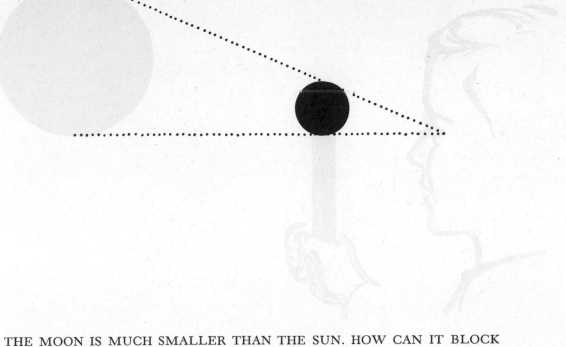

THE MOON IS MUCH SMALLER THAN THE SUN. HOW CAN IT BLOCK
OUT THE SUN?

Cut a circle or disk about one inch in diameter out of black paper.
Now cut another circle or disk about twelve inches in diameter out of
yellow paper. Fasten the yellow disk to a bulletin board or wall about
as high as you are tall. Fasten the little black disk to the end of a
ruler so that it stands up as you see in the picture. Now hold the ruler
so that the end opposite from the black disk is just above your upper
lip. Stand a few feet from the yellow disk and point the ruler so
that the black disk is just in front of the yellow one. Walk backwards
slowly until the black disk appears to cover the yellow disk, when you
look at it with one eye closed. You are probably now standing about
fourteen feet from the yellow disk. Move the ruler slowly back and forth
so that the black disk moves back and forth across the yellow disk.

This is why the moon can cover up the sun. Although the moon
is much smaller than the sun, it can black out the sun because the sun is
so much farther away. If you really made a moon and sun disk in
proportion to each other you would need to make the diameter of the
sun disk more than 400 times the diameter of the moon disk. Think
how far you would need to stand from the sun disk so that the moon
disk would cover it up. This should help you understand something
about eclipses too.

33

WHAT CAUSES AN ECLIPSE OF THE SUN?

Find two balls—one of them about four inches in diameter and another about one inch in diameter. Now find two knitting needles and put one of the balls on the end of one of the needles and the other ball on the end of the other needle.

You will need either a flash light or the light from a projector. Darken the room and turn on the flashlight or projector light. Hold the larger ball in the light and let it represent the earth. The light represents the sun. Now hold the smaller ball, which we let represent the moon, between the model of the earth and the light so that it causes a shadow on the earth model. This shows what happens when there is an eclipse of the sun. We have an eclipse when the moon moves between the sun and the earth and casts a shadow on the earth. This also helps you to understand why an eclipse is only seen on certain parts of the earth at a time.

34

WHAT CAUSES AN ECLIPSE OF THE MOON?

You can better understand what causes an eclipse of the moon by using the same balls and light which you used when you discovered what caused an eclipse of the sun. This time move the model of the moon until it is in the shadow of the earth, and now you have an eclipse of the moon. We do not have an eclipse of the moon every time the moon moves about the earth. You can discover the reason for this by moving the model of the moon slowly upward. You will notice soon that there is no eclipse because the moon is no longer in the earth's shadow. Try moving the model of the moon slowly downward and you will discover the same thing. The moon must be almost in direct line with the earth and sun for an eclipse to take place.

35

WHERE DOES THE MOON GET ITS LIGHT?

Find two balls—you could use the same two balls which you used when you were wondering about eclipses. One of the balls should be four times the diameter of the other because the earth's diameter is four times that of the moon. Take the balls and a flashlight into a darkened room. Hold the ball representing the earth between the flashlight (sun) and the ball representing the moon. Hold the moon high or low enough so that it is not in the shadow of the earth. Now you can understand why the people who are having night on the earth can see the moon. It is shining with sunlight which is reflected.

WHY CAN A WHITE MOON SOMETIMES BE SEEN IN THE DAYTIME?

Use two balls to represent the moon and the earth. You might use the same two balls which you used before. Take the two balls and a flashlight into a dark room. Hold the moon between the earth and the light which represents the sun. Now move the moon a bit to one side. You are almost sure to notice a reflection on the moon from the light on the earth which is one reason we sometimes see the moon in the daytime. The earth of course received the light from the sun.

36

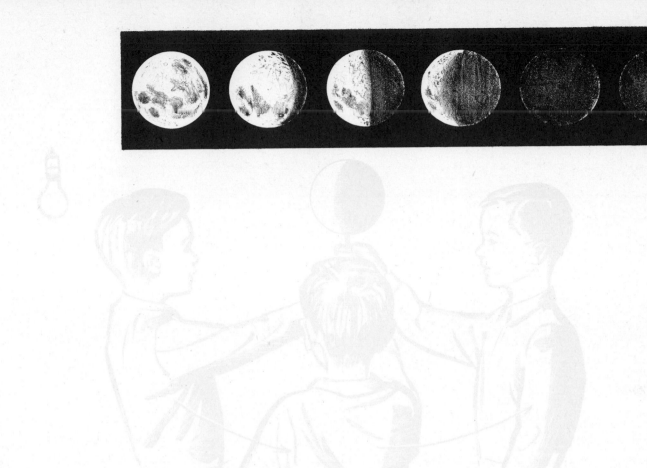

WHAT CAUSES THE PHASES OF THE MOON?

If you do this experiment to help you discover what causes the phases of the moon you will need a lighted lamp bulb and a ball. The lamp bulb will represent the sun and the ball the moon. Place the lighted lamp bulb in a darkened room above your eye level. Remember you are on the earth—now hold the ball (moon) so that you are between the sun and the moon. What do you see? You should see a full moon—the lighted side. Without moving the ball, move a little to the left—do you see the full lighted side now? Move still further. Now what do you see? As you move to your left you see less and less of the lighted side. When the moon is between you and the sun you see none of the lighted side. Keep moving and you will discover how the moon seems to again come into view. You might wish to compare what you saw with the different phases of the moon which you see in this book.

37

HOW BIG IS THE SUN?

It might help you to get a better idea of the size of the sun if you think of it in relation to the size of the earth. Everyone knows something about the size of the earth. Make a green circle about one-eighth inch in diameter on a piece of paper to represent the earth. About three and three-fourths inches from the green circle place a big period to represent the moon. The moon is about one-fourth the diameter of the earth and about 240,000 miles away from it. The sun has a diameter more than a hundred times greater than that of the earth. Make a yellow circle thirteen inches in diameter to represent the sun. Its size is then in relation to that of the earth. Place it about eight-five feet from the earth. These eight-five feet represent the 93,000,000 miles. Now you will have some idea of how far away the sun is and also how big it is in relation to the earth.

HOW DO THE PLANETS IN OUR SOLAR SYSTEM COMPARE IN SIZES AND DISTANCES?

The numbers below give the information but it is hard to imagine just how big these numbers really are. Suppose you made a clay ball

NAME OF PLANET	MERCURY	VENUS	EARTH	MARS
DIAMETER IN MILES	3,100	7,600	7,900	4,220
DISTANCE FROM SUN IN MILES	36,000,000	67,000,000	93,000,000	142,000,000

about one-fourth inch in diameter to represent the earth. Another clay ball almost the same size could stand for Venus. For Mercury and Pluto you could make clay balls only half as large as the ones you made for the earth. A clay ball to represent Mars would need to be a little larger than Mercury and not so big as earth. A couple of big marbles could represent Uranus and Neptune — their diameters should be about four times that of the earth. A baseball would be about the right size to stand for Jupiter and a tennis ball would do very well for Saturn. Now you will need a sun. You probably can't find a ball big enough to stand for the sun. You might then cut a circle about thirty inches in diameter to represent the sun. The balls or planets can be arranged in the correct order from the sun. You will not be able to use the same scale for the distances which you used for the diameters because if you did you would need to travel almost two miles to put them in place. You might place Mercury one inch from the sun and each of the other planets in relation to it — Venus two inches — and the earth three inches. Mars would be four and one-half inches. Jupiter is between three and four times as far from the sun as Mars is and Saturn is twice the distance of Jupiter. This would make Jupiter around fifteen inches and Saturn thirty inches from the sun. Uranus would be twice Saturn's distance, sixty inches or five feet. Neptune is approximately one and one-half times the distance of Uranus or seven and one-half feet. Pluto, the very farthest away from the sun, would be about ten feet.

Think of what you know about distances on the earth and this should help you to understand how very great the distances are out in space. You must remember, too, that you have been thinking only of our own solar system. There are many other stars (the sun is the only star in our solar system) and many other solar systems too.

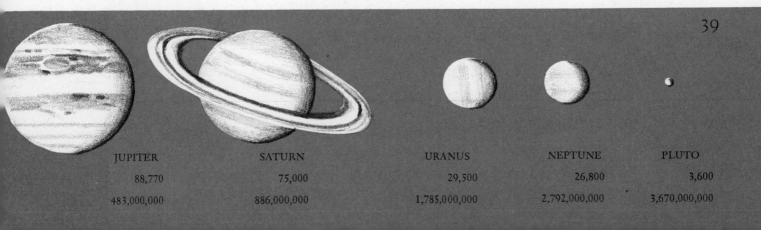

JUPITER	SATURN	URANUS	NEPTUNE	PLUTO
88,770	75,000	29,500	26,800	3,600
483,000,000	886,000,000	1,785,000,000	2,792,000,000	3,670,000,000

CEPHEUS

CASSIOPEIA'S
CHAIR

POLARIS

DRACO

URSA MINOR

URSA MAJOR

HOW CAN I RECOGNIZE SOME OF THE COMMON CONSTELLATIONS?

Some of the more common constellations are pictured on this page.
It also tells you where and when you could expect to find them. There
are some things which you might do that would help you to know
them and to recognize them when you see them in the sky.

Save empty detergent cans or other can of the same size and shape.
Wash them and allow them to dry. Now pour some black paint into
the cans from one to another and be sure that the paint covers the
whole inside before you pour the rest out. This black paint prevents
reflections later on. Now, if you wish, you might paint the cans on the
outside to make them more attractive. Set a can on a piece of white paper
and draw a line around it making a circle. Draw the constellation on the
circle and then make a pin-hole for each star. Now cut the circle out
and tape it lightly to the bottom of the can with the pencil mark side
toward the can. Use a hammer and small nail and make a hole in the
can underneath each of the pin-holes which represent stars. Bigger
holes can be made for the bigger stars. Now remove the paper from
the bottom of the can. Lift the can and look into it holding the bottom
toward the light. You should see a constellation. Point the can in the
position in which you expect to find the constellation and you will know
better what to look for the next time you are out constellation hunting.

40

SPIRAL GALAXY, FROM THE SIDE

NOW
YOU
KNOW
THAT:

Astronomy is the study of the sun, moon, stars, planets and other bodies in the universe.

The moon is smaller than the sun. But the sun is much, much farther away.

In an eclipse of the sun, the moon moves between the sun and the earth and casts a shadow on the earth.

We have an eclipse of the moon when the moon moves into the shadow of the earth.

The moon shines with reflected sunlight.

The moon has phases. We do not always see the full lighted side of it.

The diameter of the sun is about 100 times bigger than the diameter of the earth.

The sun is about 93,000,000 miles away.

There are vast distances in space.

Many stars can be seen. But the sun is the only star in our solar system.

41

MAGNETISM

42

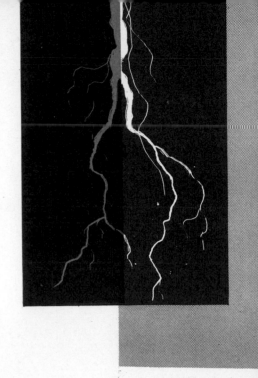

IN HIGH SCHOOL MANY BOYS AND GIRLS STUDY PHYSICS. WHEN THEY STUDY PHYSICS THEY LEARN ABOUT MANY THINGS WHICH ARE IN THEIR ENVIRONMENT, INCLUDING MAGNETISM AND ELECTRICITY. PEOPLE IN COLLEGE SOMETIMES BECOME SPECIALISTS IN THESE BRANCHES OF PHYSICS. THESE BRANCHES ARE CALLED ELECTRONICS AND ELECTRO-MAGNETISM. YOU DO NOT NEED TO WAIT UNTIL YOU ARE IN HIGH SCHOOL OR COLLEGE TO LEARN ABOUT ELECTRONICS AND ELECTRO-MAGNETISM. YOU CAN DISCOVER SOME THINGS ABOUT THEM NOW.

& ELECTRICITY

43

HOW MANY THINGS IN YOUR ROOM WILL A MAGNET ATTRACT?

Take your magnet and go about your room touching things lightly with it. If you can feel a pull when you try to take the magnet away you know that your magnet is attracting what it is touching or something near to what it is touching. If you go around the room again and look carefully at the things which your magnet attracted you will probably notice that it attracted metal things. If you look carefully again you will probably notice that it did not attract some of the metal things. It only attracted the things made of iron or steel. This is true about magnets. They attract iron and steel. There are a few other metals which magnets will attract but they are not very common.

44

WHY WILL A MAGNET SEEM TO ATTRACT SOME THINGS WHICH ARE NOT MADE OF IRON OR STEEL?

You can find an answer to this question by putting some paper clips, which your magnet is sure to pick up, under a piece of glass. Will the magnet attract through the glass and pull the clips to it? Try this same experiment with materials other than glass. You might try a piece of paper and a piece of cloth. Try some other metals such as a copper penny and silver dime. Now you know that your magnet appeared to attract some things only because there was a piece of iron or steel on the other side of them.

WILL MAGNETS ATTRACT THROUGH WATER?

This is an easy question to answer and you can probably predict what the answer will be. Here is one way to find out whether your prediction is correct but you may wish to plan a way of your own. Put a few paper clips in a glass bowl or beaker. Now fill the glass bowl or beaker about three-fourths full of water. Hold your magnet over the water and slowly lower the magnet into it. At some point along the way the clips will jump toward the magnet and cling. Was your prediction correct?

WHY CAN MAGNETS PULL ON THINGS WHICH ARE NOT TOUCHING THEM?

You may wonder how magnets can attract things which they are
not touching. Place a bar magnet on the table. Place a paper over it.
Now sprinkle some iron filings over the paper above the magnet. Tap the
paper a bit and the iron filings will form a pattern very much like the
one in the picture. You will notice lines of iron filings from the N pole to
the S pole. These filings are arranged along what are called the magnetic
lines of force. Magnets can pull on things which they are not touching
because of the magnetic lines of force.

ARE THERE MAGNETIC LINES OF FORCE BETWEEN TWO MAGNETS?

You can plan a way to do an experiment to answer this question
yourself. You might do it this way. Lay one magnet down on the table and
lay another so that an N pole and an S pole are about one-half inch apart.
The two magnets should be in a straight line with each other. Cover
them with a piece of glass and sprinkle iron filings on the glass over the
magnets. Tap the glass and see the pattern the iron filings take. The ends
of the two magnets are attracting each other — the lines of force go
from one magnet to the other. Do the same thing with paper and notice
whether the same thing happens. Try this same thing but this time arrange
the two magnets with two S poles together. Were they attracting each
other? It is easy to see that they were not attracting each other — they

46

were pushing away or repelling as it is called. Try this again and use the two N poles. You are almost sure to predict that the lines of force will show that they repel and you will be right. You may wish to try this over again to see whether the same things always happen.

This experiment will remind you of the laws of poles of magnets.

Unlike poles always attract each other.

Like poles repel each other.

There is a simpler way of saying the same thing.

An N pole and an S pole attract each other.

Two N poles repel each other.

Two S poles repel each other.

If you have never experimented with the magnets before you may wish to try out the laws of poles by putting an N and S pole together and feeling the pull. When you put like poles together you will feel the push.

CAN YOU MAKE USE OF WHAT YOU KNOW ABOUT MAGNETS?

Arrange three bar magnets end to end leaving about one-half inch between each of them. Two of them should be turned over or not marked so that you do not know where the N and S poles are. The N and S poles should be known on one of the end magnets. Place a paper over the magnets so that the far end of each one shows. Now sprinkle iron filings on the paper over the magnets. Tap the paper and try to decide what the unknown poles are from the kind of pattern which the iron filings form. Now examine the magnets and see whether you were right. Were you?

47

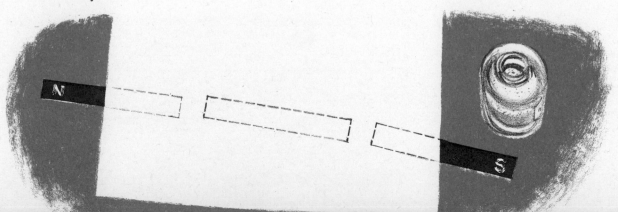

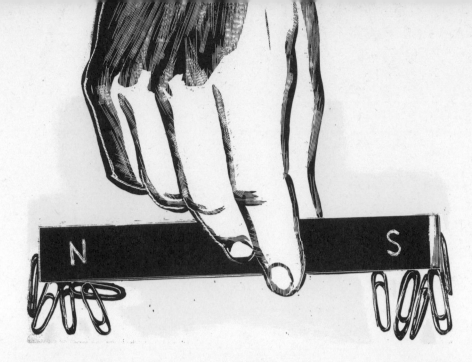

WHAT HAPPENS WHEN A MAGNET IS BROKEN—IS IT NO LONGER A MAGNET?

Do this experiment only if you have a magnet which you are willing to break. Check your magnet and see about how many paper clips it will pick up. Check your magnet to see which end is the N pole and which is the S pole. Now break the magnet in as nearly the center as you can. Check each half of your magnet. How many paper clips would it pick up? How many paper clips would the other half pick up? Check the ends of the two halves — are they N and S poles? Are the broken ends the same or different poles? You have doubtless decided that you have two magnets but neither of the magnets are as strong as the original one was. You have probably also decided that the broken ends are opposite poles.

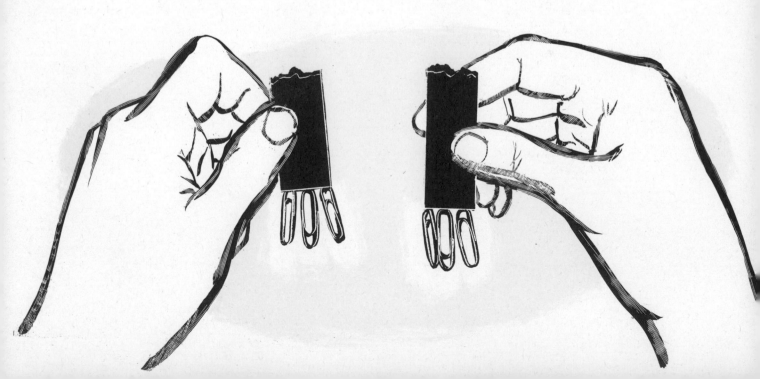

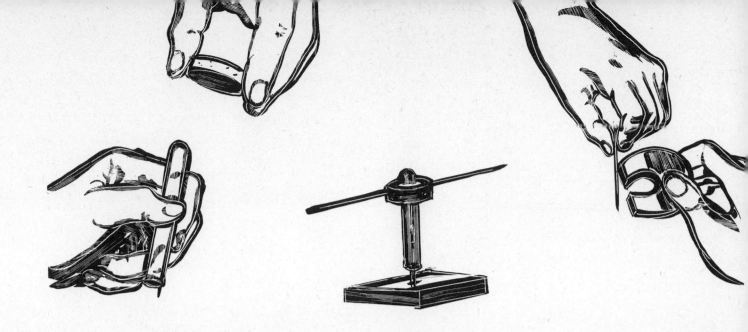

HOW CAN I MAKE A COMPASS?

Find a cork about one-half inch thick and about one and one-half inches in diameter. Into the middle of the cork put the closed end of a small glass test tube or glass bottle. Now find a piece of wood about four inches square and about one-half inch thick. Pound a nail through the middle of the wood so that it stands straight up about two or more inches. Use scotch tape and tape the eye end of a needle to the nail so that the point of the needle is an inch or more above the nail. Now the bottle which is in the cork can be turned over the point of the needle. The bottle should turn freely. You are now ready to make two magnets out of two steel darning needles. You will make the magnets by magnetizing the darning needles.

Magnetize the darning needles by rubbing the point of the needle on the S pole of a permanent magnet. The rubbing should be done in one direction only and approximately 50 times. Place one needle in the cork by pushing the point into the cork about one-fourth inch. Place the other needle in the cork directly opposite to the first needle. This needle should be put in eye first. Now place the bottle which is in the cork over the point of the needle. The magnetized darning needles should act as a compass needle.

The N pole of a magnet is the north-seeking pole. The S pole is the south-seeking pole of a magnet.

49

HOW DO ELECTRIC MAGNETS WORK?

Before you can find out about how electric magnets work you need to make a couple of them. To make one you should find a bolt about 2 inches long, which you are very sure is iron, and four or more yards of cotton-covered copper wire. Wrap the wire neatly around the bolt from one end to the other and back again. You may have enough wire to make three layers of it on the bolt. You should leave about one foot at each end of the wire which you wrapped around the bolt so that you will have something to connect to a dry cell. After you have finished wrapping the wire around the bolt, twist the two wires together so that it cannot come loose. Now you are ready to find out how it works.

Try using your wrapped bolt to pick up paper clips. Could you do it? Now connect one of the wires to one post of a dry cell. Be sure you have pushed the cotton back from the end of the wire so it is bare before you make the connection. Connect the other wire to the other post of the dry cell. Find out whether your electric magnet will pick up the paper clips. Does it? Take one of the wires from one of the dry cell posts. Do the paper clips drop? Try this same experiment but use nails instead of paper clips. You are correct if you say that your electric magnet works only when electricity is going through it. This is why it is called an electro-magnet.

50

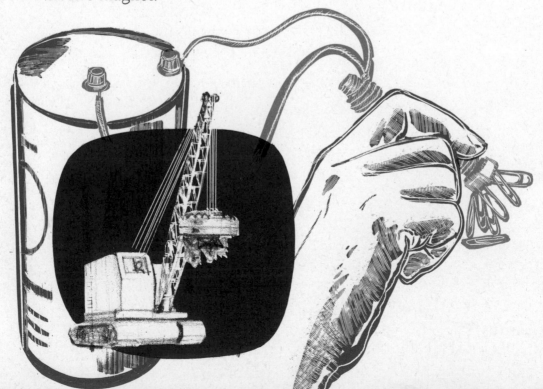

Use a light-weight iron rod about 12 inches long. Bend it in a U shape and wind it with cotton-covered copper wire, as shown in the picture. Begin at the bottom of one arm and wind about 3 layers on this arm. Then, without winding the top of the U, carry the wire across to the other arm and wind as shown in the picture. Leave about a foot of wire at each end for connections. Bolts on the ends of the U or wrapping with tape will keep the wire from slipping off. Remove ¼ inch of insulation from the ends of the wire and connect to a dry cell as shown.

When wrapped correctly, one end of the horseshoe magnet should be an N pole and the other end an S pole.

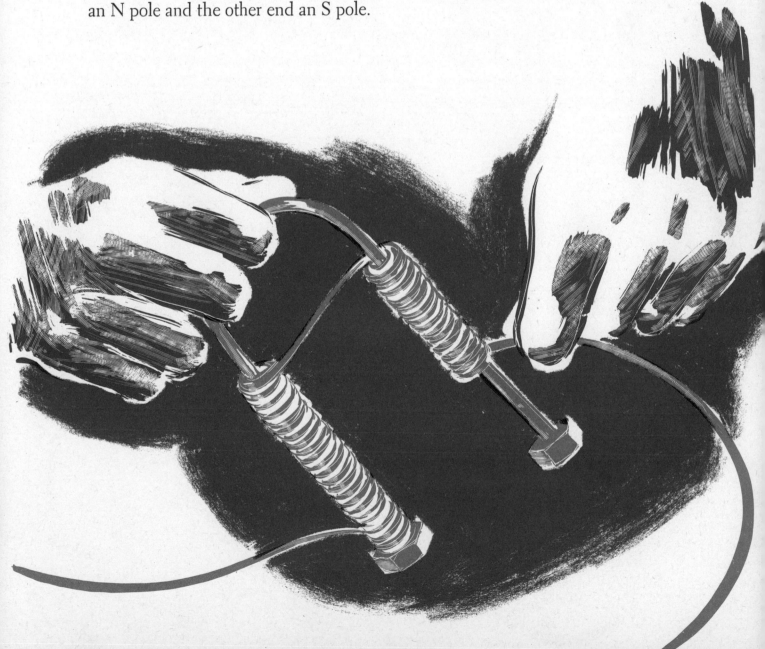

Use a piece of your copper wire with the insulation removed from the ends of it. Bend the wire as shown and fasten to a flashlight battery with rubber bands. Attach one end of the wire to a flashlight bulb and adjust so that the tip of the bulb touches the center terminal of the battery. Use the free end of the wire as a switch by touching the bottom of the battery with it. Electricity going through the threadlike wire of the bulb causes it to become hot and give off light.

52

You may wonder what is inside of a dry cell and whether a dry cell is really dry. If you have an old dry cell which is no longer a good one, open it and see what you find in it.

Put paper on the floor and place the dry cell on it. Use a hammer and large screw driver to open the dry cell around the top and down the side. When it is open spread the sides apart so you can see what is inside. Look carefully and see whether you can find each of the parts in the picture. You should find a zinc can which is lined with a heavy paper saturated with chemicals. You should also find a carbon rod and a black mixture that has chemicals in it. The chemicals are powdered manganese dioxide and ammonium chloride solution. You will probably notice that one post is connected to the carbon rod and the other to the zinc can. The parts are all held in by wax and the outside covered with paper. The liquid then cannot get out and the outside of the dry cell is really dry.

The chemicals, zinc and carbon are very important parts of a dry cell in producing electricity.

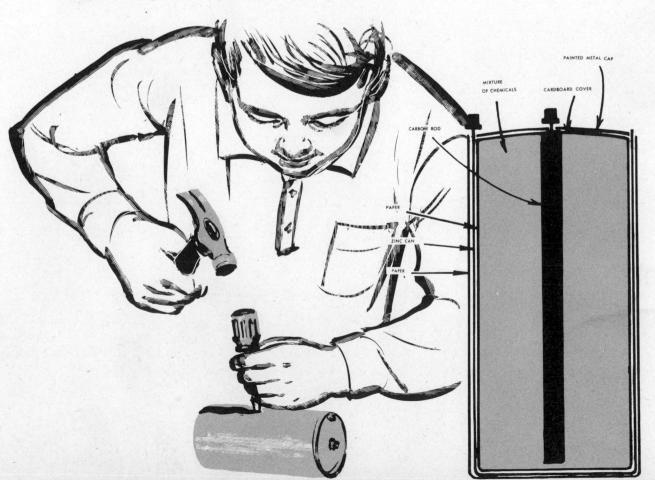

53

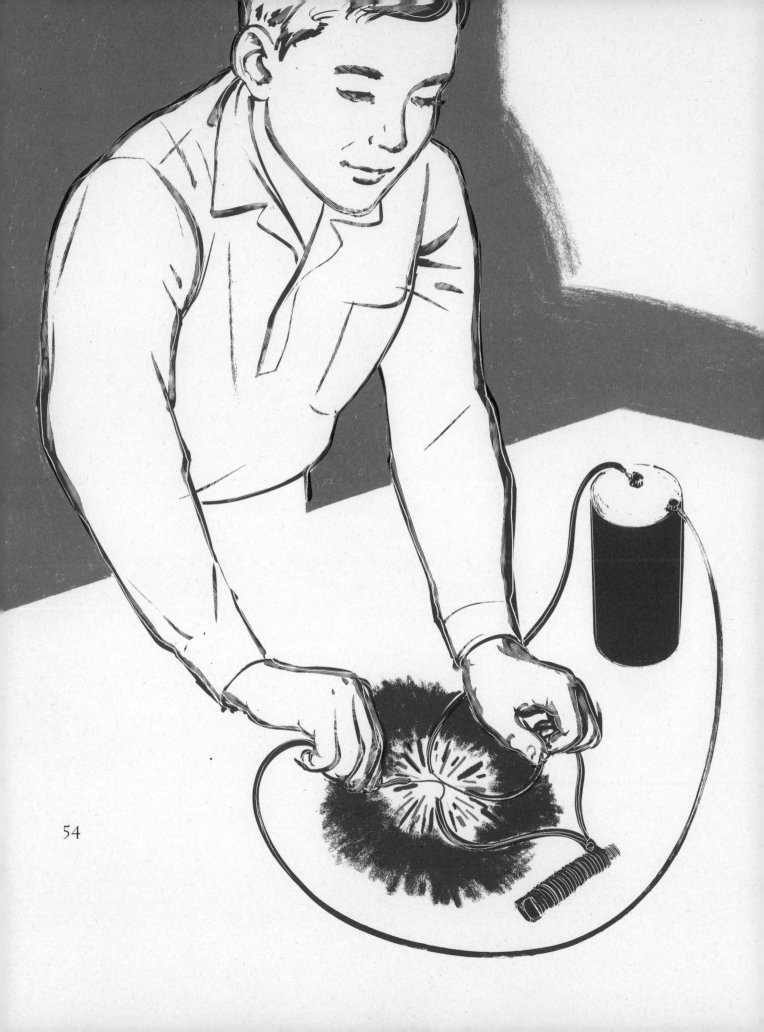

54

WHEN IS ELECTRICITY DANGEROUS?

To help you understand why electricity is sometimes dangerous you may want to use a dry cell and the electro-magnet which you made. When we do experiments it is good to use a dry cell because it is not powerful enough to be very dangerous, but even with dry cells it is not wise to make a mistake in wiring.

You remember that to make your electro-magnet work you had to have both wires connected to the posts of the dry cell. This made a complete circuit. Electricity can go through the wire only when there is a complete circuit. If you cut one of the wires leading to the dry cell you would then have a broken circuit. Electricity could not go where the wire was cut unless the ends of the wires touched each other.

There is a kind of circuit which can be very dangerous. You can discover for yourself why. Connect the wires of your electric magnet to the posts of the dry cell. Now take some of the cotton covering off of each of the wires which lead to the dry cell so that there is a small bare place on each one. Place the wires so that the two bare spots will touch each other. Notice what happens. Can you see anything? Can you feel anything? Now you have discovered what can cause a fire. This is a short circuit.

The covering on wiring is very important. It helps keep the electricity on the right path. Electricity cannot travel through some kinds of materials such as cotton, rubber, etc. They are called non-conductors and are used as insulation on wires.

Electricity is dangerous when the wiring is poor and electricity is permitted to go the wrong paths. It is a safe practice always to be sure that wires have no broken places in their covering, the insulation. It is also a safe practice to never touch electric wires which you are not sure about.

55

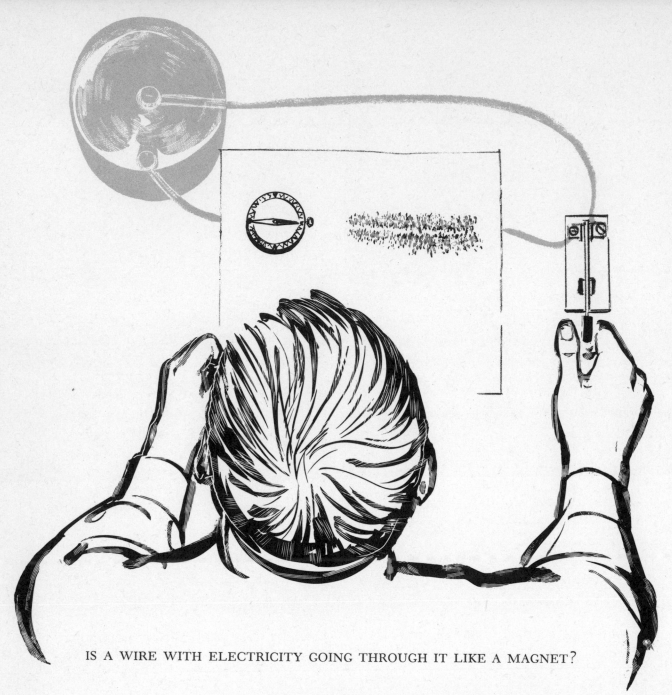

IS A WIRE WITH ELECTRICITY GOING THROUGH IT LIKE A MAGNET?

Wire in a circuit a dry cell and a switch. When the switch is closed electricity will be going through the wire. Remember to leave the switch closed only when you are experimenting. Scatter a few iron filings on a paper. Move the paper with iron filings on it under the wire while the switch is open. Now close the switch — open it again. You probably discovered that the wire acts as a magnet when electricity is going through it. Now move a compass under the wire and again open and close the switch. Did the needle in the compass act as though a magnet had been brought close to it? It should.

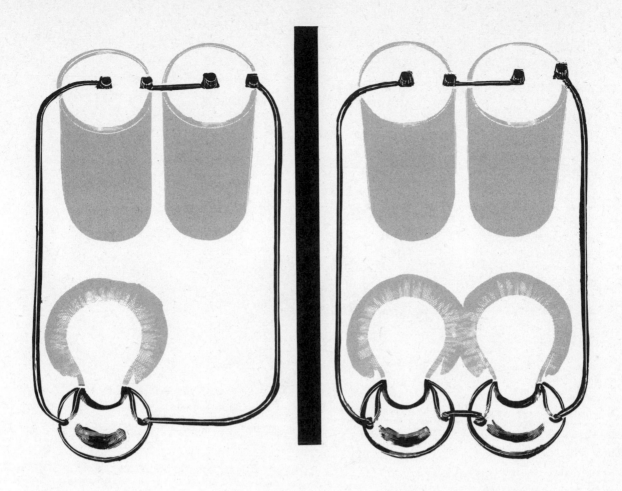

WHEN THERE IS ONE LIGHT BULB IN A CIRCUIT HOW CAN ANOTHER
BE ADDED?

If you have a light bulb in a circuit it probably looks like the picture
on this page. Another light bulb can be added very easily. Remove a
wire from one of the socket posts of the light bulb in the circuit, and
fasten the wire to the socket post of the light bulb which you wish to add.
Now all you need to do is use another wire and connect the socket posts
of the two light bulbs. Try out your circuit with two light bulbs in it.
Did both light bulbs light? They should. Was the light from each of them
as bright as when there was only one in the circuit? Probably not. What
happened when you screwed one of the light bulbs out? The other light
bulb went out because you had broken the circuit. Now you understand
about some Christmas tree lights. They are like this. They are connected in
series. You might add more light bulbs to your series and see
what happens.

57

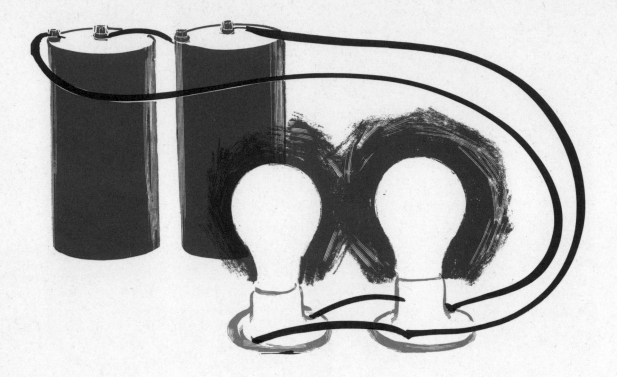

HOW CAN TWO LIGHT BULBS BE PUT IN A CIRCUIT SO THAT IF ONE GOES OUT THE OTHER STAYS ON?

You have discovered something about a connection in series. Now try this. Connect up one light bulb so that it is in a complete circuit. Place another light bulb close to the first one and connect one post of one bulb socket to one post of the other bulb socket. Now connect the other two posts in the same way. One of the bulb sockets will have four wires connected to it and this is all right. Now try your circuit. Did the light bulbs light up? Were they less bright, brighter or the same as when there was only one bulb? Find out what happens when one of the bulbs is taken out. Did the other one stay bright? This is called a parallel connection. In a parallel connection each bulb operates independently from the others. It then is as bright as before and when one burns out the others stay on. You might discover for yourself what happens when three, four or more bulbs are connected in parallel.

58

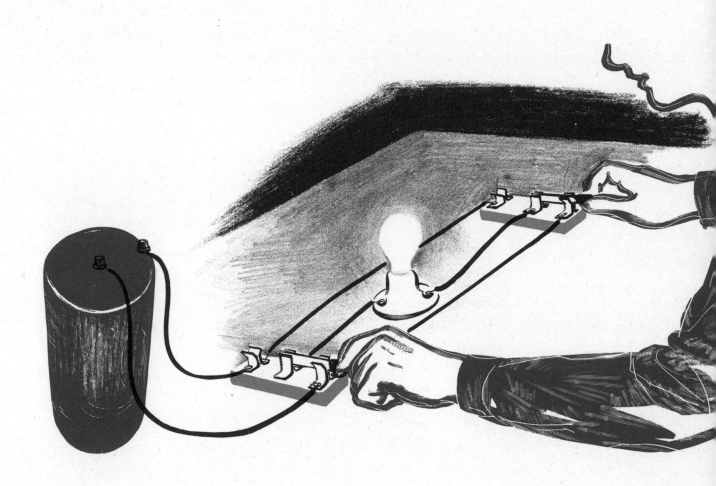

HOW IS A LIGHT WIRED SO THAT IT MAY BE TURNED OFF AND ON AT
TWO PLACES?

If you will get a light bulb, two double-throw knife switches,
insulated wire and a dry cell you can discover for yourself how a light can
be turned on and off at two different places. Connect the center posts of
both double-throw switches to the light bulb socket. Now connect the
outside posts of the switches to each other. It is easy now to see where to
connect the dry cell. The outside posts on one of the switches will have
two wires on them. Try out your connection. Did it work?

59

To make a telegraph set you must first make an electric magnet. In addition to the electro-magnet you will need a block of wood about four inches wide, six inches long and one inch thick. You will also need a dry cell, a few short nails, some insulated wire and two strips of metal about four inches long and one-half inch wide. The metal can be cut from the sides of a tin can.

Make a hole in the block of wood so the electro-magnet can be mounted upright in it. This hole should be about one inch from one end and one inch from one side of the block of wood. Now nail one end of one of the strips of metal to the same end of the block of wood but in the opposite corner from the electro-magnet. The metal strip can then be bent so that the free end of it is over the top end of the electric magnet. The metal should be close to the magnet but not touching it. One end of the other strip of metal can be nailed to the opposite end of the board. The strip of metal should be bent upward and a nail put in the board under it. This will serve as a switch.

Now connect up your telegraph set. Connect one of the wires from the electro-magnet to the dry cell. Connect the other wire from the dry cell to the end of the strip of metal which is fast to the board and serves as a switch. Connect the other wire from the electro-magnet to the nail which is under the end of metal which is the switch.

Push down on the metal strip so that it touches the nail. This should make a complete circuit and cause the electro-magnet to pull the metal which is above down with a clicking sound. Remove your finger and the metal strip should spring up breaking the circuit. Then the electro-magnet is no longer a magnet and the other strip of metal is released. Your set may need a little adjusting but you should soon be able to use it.

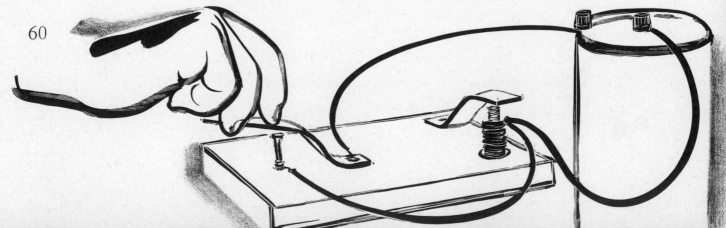

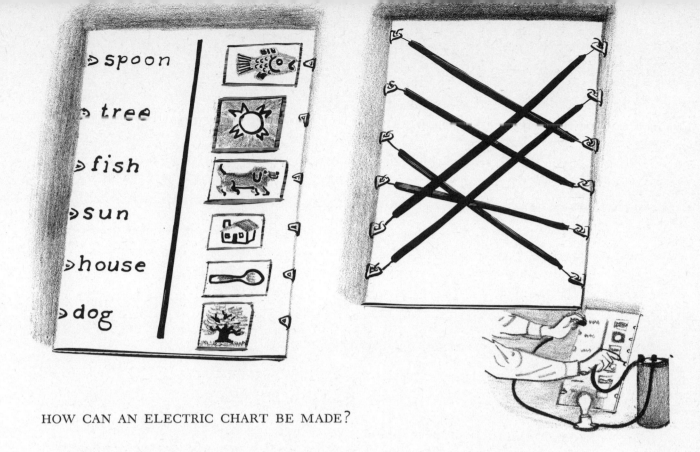

HOW CAN AN ELECTRIC CHART BE MADE?

You can make an electric chart which will appear a great deal like the one in the picture if you have a heavy cardboard, paper fasteners, insulated wire, a light bulb and a dry cell. Of course you will need pictures and matching names. Be sure your paper fasteners are good conductors of electricity.

Arrange the pictures on the cardboard in a neat order. Arrange the names on the cardboard along one side or across the bottom. When the pictures and names have been mounted in place you are ready to put in the paper fasteners and do the wiring. The wire will need to be stretched on the back of the cardboard from the paper fastener under the picture to the paper fastener by the correct name and fastened securely.

Connect up the light bulb with a dry cell. Put a fairly long wire on the other post of the dry cell and another on the other post of the light bulb socket. Now you are ready to find out whether your chart works. Stand the chart in front of you. Test the chart by placing the free end of one wire on the head of the paper fastener under a picture and by placing the free end of the other wire on the head of the paper fastener by the correct name. Did it work? Did the light bulb light? If it did then your chart is ready to use.

61

HOW CAN A SWITCH BE MADE SO THAT TWO THINGS MAY BE TURNED ON AT THE SAME TIME?

Find a block of wood about two inches wide, three inches long, and one inch thick. You will need another piece of wood about two inches long and one-half inch wide and thick. Mark a place for a screw on each corner of the larger piece of wood. Be sure to use screws which are good conductors of electricity because they will become the posts. Now you will need two strips of metal (copper if possible) one-half inch wide, and three inches long. Tack one end of each of these strips to the long piece of wood like this. The wood will be the handle.

Place the ends of the metal strips over the screw marks in the corners of the wood block. You are ready to put in the screws. On one end the screws go through the metal strips and into the wood. At the other end they go directly into the wood. Screw them down far enough that only a wire can be put under them.

You should now be able to use your switch to turn on two things at a time, a light and a bell, for instance. To close the switch you take a hold of the small wood cross piece or handle and pull the metal strips sideway so that they touch each of the heads of the screws. To open the switch you push them sideway off of the screw heads. Try out your switch. Have you discovered that a double-pole, simple throw-switch is almost the same as two single-throw switches side by side? Have you discovered that you can use one side without the other?

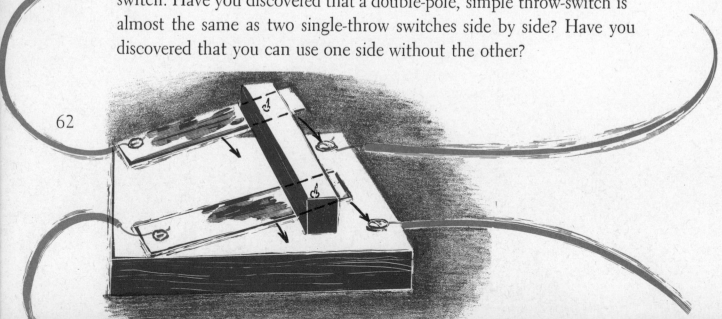

WHAT IS STATIC ELECTRICITY?

The electricity you have been experimenting and working with is current electricity. The lightning you see in the sky is another kind — it is static or frictional electricity. Here is a way you can make static or frictional electricity work for you. Blow up several balloons. Rub them vigorously on a woolen cloth. Place them against the wall and notice what they do. This is because the balloons have a charge of static electricity. They then attract the wall which has no charge of electricity.

HOW CAN I MAKE A SIMPLE ELECTROSCOPE?

An electroscope is an instrument for detecting the presence of an electric charge on a body or for telling whether the charge is positive or negative.

Cut a strip of tissue paper 2 inches wide and about 18 inches long. Crease it in the middle and rub it with a piece of fur or flannel. Hang it over a pencil and bring your hand up between the two pieces. Rub a plastic comb with the fur or flannel and bring it between the leaves of the paper. Did the same thing happen?

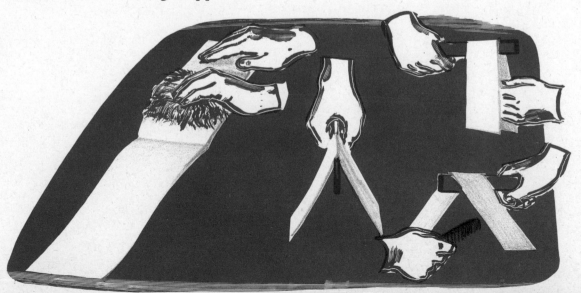

63

CAN YOU MAKE A PING PONG BALL ROLL WITH ELECTRICITY?

Rub a hard rubber rod (a rubber comb might do) with a woolen cloth. Place the ping pong ball on a table and hold the rubber rod toward it. What does the ball do? It will probably roll toward the rod. It is attracted toward the hard rubber rod because of the charge of electricity in the rod. The ping pong ball, of course, has no charge.

HOW CAN A PIECE OF FOIL BE MADE TO FLY?

Find a very, very thin piece of aluminum foil. Rub the rubber rod with the woolen cloth and touch it to a small piece of aluminum foil. At first the aluminum foil will cling closely to the rod. Soon it will become charged with the same kind of charge which the hard rubber rod has and will then be easily shaken loose. Now you can chase the aluminum foil about the room with your rubber rod. This can happen because the aluminum foil and the rubber rod now repel each other.

NOW
YOU
KNOW
THAT:

Physics includes the study of magnets and electricity.

Magnets attract things made of iron and steel.

Magnets attract iron and steel even through materials such as paper, cloth, glass and water.

Magnets have magnetic lines of force.

A magnet has an "N" pole and an "S" pole.

With two magnets, unlike poles attract, like poles repel.

A broken magnet becomes two magnets, each with an "N" and "S" pole.

An electric magnet works only when electricity is going through the wire of which it is made.

Electric magnets have poles and magnetic fields around them.

Poles of an electric magnet can be reversed.

Electricity can be dangerous.

Frictional and static electricity are the same.

Electro-magnets are important in equipment such as telegraph sets.

Like charges of electricity repel and unlike charges attract.

Insulation on wire is important. It prevents electricity going where it is not wanted.

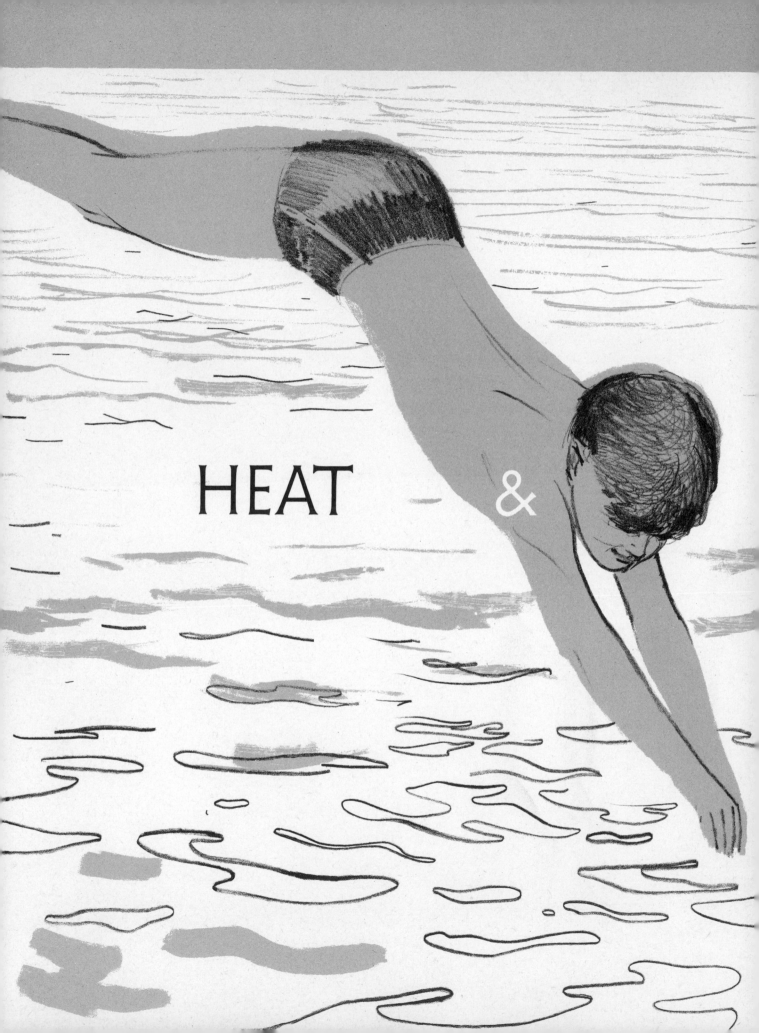

HEAT &

WHEN SCIENTISTS STUDY HEAT AND WHAT IT CAN DO THEY ARE STUDYING A BRANCH OF PHYSICS. IT IS CALLED THERMODYNAMICS. THE EXPERIMENTS AND ACTIVITIES WHICH FOLLOW ARE ALL USEFUL IN MAKING DISCOVERIES ABOUT HEAT AND WHAT IT DOES.

COLD

WHAT HAPPENS TO WATER WHEN IT IS HEATED?

Fill a flask almost full of cold water. Add some vegetable coloring so that you can see it easily. Put a rubber stopper which has a glass tube in it in the flask and push it in firmly. There should be just enough water so that it will come about one-half way up in the tube. Now set the flask in a pan of hot water. As the water cools in the pan add more hot water. Watch the water in the glass tube. You will discover that as the water in the flask gets warmer it will move farther up the tube. This is because water takes up more room when it is heated. It expands.

DOES WARM WATER WEIGH LESS THAN COLD WATER?

Use the flask and rubber stopper that you used in the last experiment. Fill the flask with ice-cold water. Put the rubber stopper in firmly so that the cold water fills the glass tube clear to the top. Now weigh the flask full of cold water. Use a balance scale and gram weight if you have them. Set the flask in a dish of hot water. As the hot water cools add more hot water. When the water in the flask becomes warm and expands the water will rise in the tube and run over the top. As soon as the water stops running out of the top of the glass tube remove the flask, wipe it dry and weigh it again. You will discover that it weighs several grams lighter now than it did the first time. It is just as full of water though. It weighs less because the water expanded and some of it ran out. Warm water is lighter than cold water.

DO METALS EXPAND WHEN THEY ARE HEATED?

Get a brass curtain rod about two feet long. Rest it on two pieces of wood as you see in the picture so that it is about four inches from the table. Be sure that one end of it is against a wall or solid surface. Put a piece of rubber or a piece of a balloon over the neck of a milk bottle and fasten with a rubber band. The rubber should be stretched slightly. Rest the milk bottle on its side so that the end of the metal rod just lightly touches the rubber but does not push on it. Arrange candles under the metal rod and light them. Watch the rubber carefully. What do you think you see happen to the rubber? The metal rod probably begins pushing on it. It has become longer because the heat causes it to expand.

Put the candles out and allow the rod to cool. Again look carefully at the rubber on the milk bottle. Has there been another change? As the rod cools it shortens, contracts. Now it is not pushing on the rubber so hard.

69

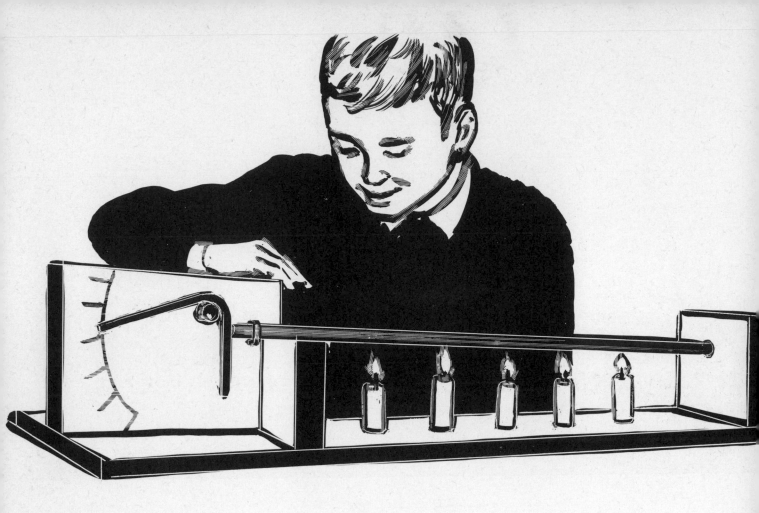

HOW CAN WE MAKE EXPANSION WORK FOR US?

You can make a thermostat like the one in the picture. The big board should be about two and one-half feet long and four inches wide. The metal rod can be the one you used in the last experiment. The other metal rod, the pointer rod, should be one-fourth inch square and about eight inches long. You will need to bend it. Now you can put these parts together. The long rod is inserted in a shallow hole in the small upright board. The other end of it rests under a staple in the other upright board. The small, square rod rests freely in another staple on the other upright board. When the candles under the long rod are lighted, the heat from them causes the rod to expand and push the pointer rod up. Mark a scale on the pointer-rod board. We could tell by looking at the pointer whether the long rod is hotter or colder than it was. Thermostats are used to turn equipment off and on. A thermostat in our house helps control the heat.

WHAT WILL ABSORB MORE HEAT — DARK OR LIGHT?

Place two thermometers, which read the same temperature, side
by side in the sunshine. Cover one with white paper and another with
black paper. Examine the thermometers in ten minutes and again in
another ten minutes. You will see that the thermometer covered with
black will be higher. The dark color absorbs more heat than the light one   71
and the light color reflects more heat than the dark one. Now you
can understand why people wear more dark-colored clothing in
wintertime and light-colored clothing in summertime.

HOW DOES THE TEMPERATURE OF CLEAN WATER COMPARE WITH THE
TEMPERATURE OF DIRTY WATER?

Fill two cups with water. In one of the cups stir some soil. Set
both cups aside in a cool dark place or in the refrigerator until they
are the same temperature. Now set them in the direct sunshine. Take the
temperature of each of them every ten minutes for about one-half hour.
You probably have predicted what you would find. Was your
prediction correct? What did happen? You are sure to have decided
that dirty water absorbs heat faster than clean water.

72

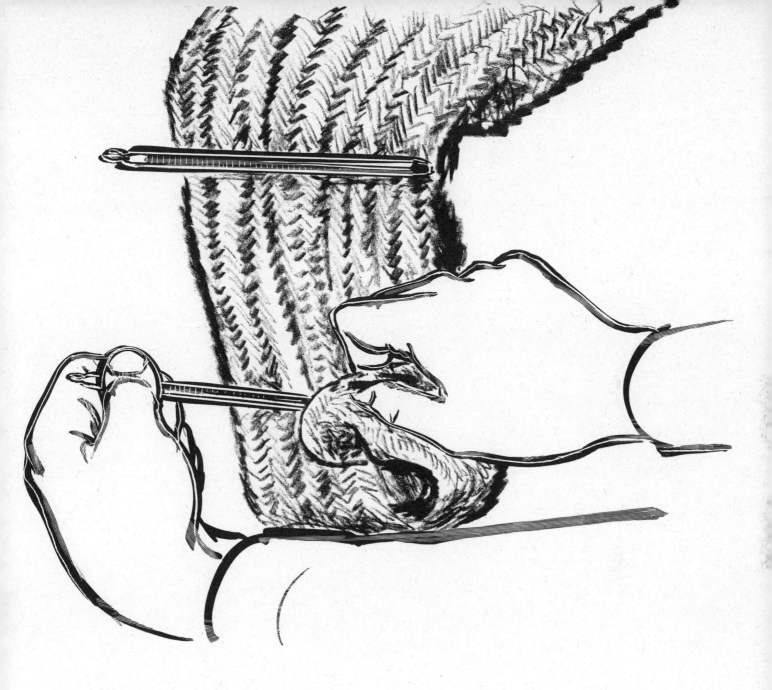

WHAT IS ANOTHER WAY TO MAKE THINGS WARM?

Use two thermometers. Place both of them on a woolen cloth
(a sweater sleeve will do). Note the temperature. They should read
the same. Allow one of them to rest close by. Use the other thermometer
and rub the bulb vigorously on the wool. Again read both
thermometers. The one which was rubbed will probably read higher.
Heat is generated by friction. Rub your two hands together and they
will feel warmer.

73

WHICH CARRIES HEAT BETTER, A METAL ROD OR A WOODEN ROD?

Find two rods which are exactly the same length and diameter.
Put water in a beaker and heat it until it boils. Put the ends of both the
rods into the water. Hold the other ends of the rods, one in the right
hand and one in the left hand. Which one could you hold longer?
Now remove the rods from the water and cool them. Switch the rods so
that the one which was in your right hand is now in your left hand.
Place them in the water again. Which heated faster this time? The
metal rod probably heated faster each time. You see, metal is a better
conductor of heat than wood is.

74   You are sure to know what would happen if you had put the ends
of the rods in a flame. The wood would start to burn. It would start
to burn because the heat could not be carried away fast enough by
such a poor conductor.

WHICH IS A BETTER CONDUCTOR OF HEAT, SILVER OR STEEL?

Heat a beaker of water until it boils hard. Put two spoons — one sterling silver, the other steel — into the boiling water. Hold the handle of one in the right hand and the handle of the other in the left hand. Which is more comfortable to hold? Which can you hold longer? Try this experiment over again but reverse the spoons. Which is more comfortable to hold and which can you hold longer? It makes no difference which hand you hold it in, the silver spoon is the first to become too hot to hold. Silver is a better conductor of heat than steel.

75

HOW HOT MUST SOMETHING BE TO BEGIN BURNING?

Find pieces of paper, cotton cloth, wood (paste sticks) and aluminum foil. Cut them into small pieces about one-fourth inch square. They should be as thin as the paper. Place a flat piece of metal (a pie tin will do) over a flame and let it get really hot. When it is hot drop one piece of each kind of material on the hottest part of the metal at the same time, and see which burns first. Do this several times. Did the same kind of material burn first each time? Did the same kind of material last longest each time? Probably paper burned first and the aluminum was left.

You probably remember that poor conductors burn more quickly. The temperature at which something burns is called its kindling point.

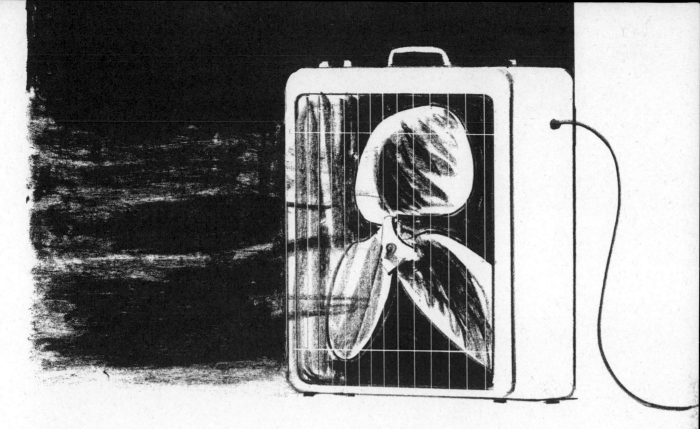

NOW
YOU
KNOW
THAT:

Study of heat and what it does is Thermodynamics, a branch of Physics.

Water expands when heated.

Warm water weighs less than the same amount of cold water.

Metal expands when heated.

We can make metal expansion work for us.

Dark-colored things absorb more heat than light-colored things.

Dirty water absorbs heat faster than clean water.

Friction generates heat.

Metal is a better conductor of heat than wood.

Some metals are better conductors of heat than others.

Wood, paper and cloth are poor conductors of heat and burn quickly.

METEOROLOGY IS A STUDY OF WEATHER. SCIENTISTS WHO SPEND
THEIR TIME STUDYING ABOUT WEATHER ARE CALLED METEOROLOGISTS.
IF IT WERE NOT FOR METEOROLOGISTS WE WOULD NOT HAVE THE KIND
OF WEATHER REPORTS WHICH WE NOW GET SEVERAL TIMES A DAY.
OF COURSE, METEOROLOGISTS SOMETIMES MAKE MISTAKES BECAUSE IT IS
DIFFICULT TO BE SURE OF WHAT WILL HAPPEN IN THE BLANKET OF
AIR WHICH IS AROUND THE EARTH. METEOROLOGISTS USE CERTAIN KINDS
OF INSTRUMENTS TO HELP THEM GET THEIR INFORMATION.

IN THIS SECTION YOU WILL DISCOVER SOME WAYS TO MAKE
INSTRUMENTS OF YOUR OWN. YOU WILL ALSO DISCOVER SOME
IMPORTANT IDEAS WHICH HELP TO EXPLAIN THE PUZZLES ABOUT
WEATHER.

WEATHER

WHAT MAKES A CLOUD?

You can make a cloud as the boy in the picture is doing. Use a warm quart milk bottle. Fill it with hot water. Now pour three fourths of the water out. After about five minutes place an ice cube over the mouth of the milk bottle and hold it there firmly.

The ice cube cools the air around it. Since the cool air is heavier it moves down and touches the warm air. The warm air is full of moisture called water vapor. As this water vapor cools, it forms little droplets and we see the moisture as a cloud in the bottle.

Now you have discovered the way clouds in the sky are formed — warm air which has much moisture in it is cooled. The moisture then collects into larger particles which make up the cloud. When moisture collects this way we call it condensation.

WHAT MAKES IT RAIN?

Bring some water in a tea kettle to a boil. Water changes to water vapor as it boils. As the water vapor hits the cool air, you can see it as steam. Now fill a glass beaker with ice cubes. The ice cubes will make the glass cold. Suppose you see what happens when you hold the beaker of ice cubes in the steam. What do you notice on the outside of the beaker? You probably see little drops of water. If you hold it long enough some of the drops of water may fall as rain. When clouds become heavy enough and cold enough they drop their moisture as rain.

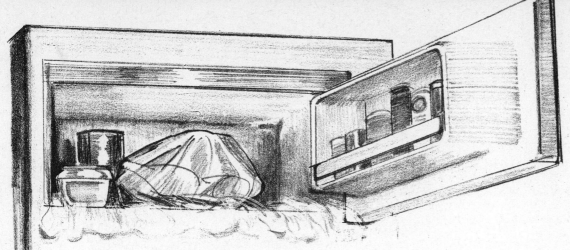

WHAT CAUSES FROST?

This is a discovery you can make by looking into the freezer section of your refrigerator. Open the door and watch what happens. Do you see a fog falling down from the opening? As you discovered earlier, water vapor condenses when it comes in contact with cold air. Some of the water vapor touched the inside of the freezer. You are almost sure to see frost there. Some of the water vapor turned to crystals of ice when it touched the cold sides of the freezer. This is what happens when water vapor touches the cold glass window panes. It freezes.

From this you can imagine what causes snow. You are right if you decide that snow is caused by water vapor freezing into ice crystals high up in the sky.

WHAT ARE SNOWFLAKES LIKE?

Wait for a day when it snows. Take a hand lens or reading glass. Put on a dark coat or a dark pair of mittens. Catch a snowflake on your sleeve and look at it carefully through the lens. Almost all snowflakes have six sides or parts. The crystals of ice are almost sure to be arranged in sixes. Look at other snowflakes and see whether you can find the six parts. Can you find two snowflakes that are alike?

81

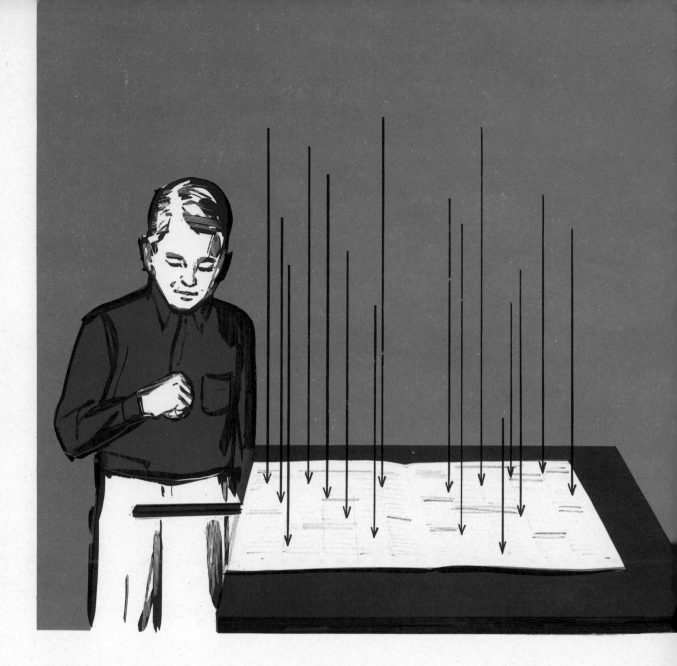

DOES AIR PUSH DOWN WITH A GREAT DEAL OF FORCE?

Place a piece of board about one inch wide and two feet long on a table with 18 inches of it on the table and 6 inches of it off the table. Cover the part of the board which is on the table with a sheet of newspaper. Now hit hard the end of the board which is off the table. What did you notice? The paper did not fly up because the air above it was holding it down. Air pushes down with a force of about 15 pounds on each square inch. If there were 720 square inches of paper, figure for yourself how great the pressure on the paper was.

82

Find a tin can that has a screw top on it. Take the top off. Put about one-half inch of water in it and set it over a fire. The water will soon boil. The water is boiling hard when you see steam coming from the can. When you see steam coming from the can you can be sure the can is almost full of steam. Now, careful not to burn yourself, take the can from the fire and screw the top on tight. Watch the can carefully. What do you see happen? The can now probably looks much like the one in the picture.

In order to explain why this happens you will need to remember:

Water turns into water vapor fast when it is heated.

Water vapor takes up more room than water does.

Water vapor will push much of the air out of the can.

When water vapor cools it condenses.

Condensed water vapor, or water, takes up less room than water vapor.

There is much less air in the can now than there was in the beginning.

There is much less air pressure on the inside of the can now than there is on the outside.

If you remember all of these important ideas you will know why the can crumpled up. The air pressure on the outside of the can caused it.

WHERE IS THE WARM AIR IN A ROOM GOING?

Cut a piece of colored construction paper into a six inch square. Find and mark the center. Draw a line from the center mark in a circular pattern always keeping it one-half inch from the line just inside of it. Your drawing should be made to look like the one in the picture. Now cut on your pencil marks almost to the center mark. You should have a spiral paper like the picture. Fasten a string to the center so you can carry your spiral paper around without touching it. Hold it over a radiator. Now hold it near the floor. Hold it a little distance above a stove. Hold it over a lighted lamp. What have you decided about where warm air goes? Warm air goes up because the cold air, which is heavier, comes down and pushes it up.

DOES WARM AIR WEIGH LESS THAN COLD AIR?

Find two tin cans of the same size and kind. Put the top on them. Now use a nail and put a small nail hole in the top of each of them. Hang a yard stick from a support so that it balances about ten inches from the table. Hang a can on each end so that they balance each other and so that they cannot slide off of the yard stick. Place on alcohol lamp under one of the cans—light it. Notice what happens. Can you explain it? The air in the one can expanded as it was heated. Some of the air then escaped through the little hole. This then explains why there was less air in one than the other even though it was full of air. It is easy to see that warm air is lighter than cold air. Winds are caused by cold air pushing in and crowding warm air away.

84

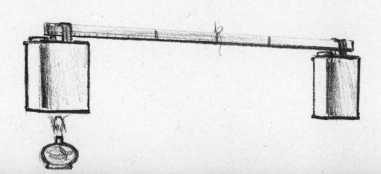

WHY ARE LAKE BREEZES SOMETIMES COLD AND SOMETIMES WARM?

Fill two paper cups—one with water and the other with damp (not wet) soil. Place them in the refrigerator overnight. The next day take the temperatures. They should be almost the same. Set them in the direct sunshine. Take the temperature of each of them every ten minutes. What do you notice? Which warms up faster, land or water? Now you have an idea why it may be too cold to go swimming even though the sand on the beach seems warm. You know, too, why we have cool breezes off the lake in the summer time. Leave the cups for several hours and take the temperatures. Did they become nearer the same temperature after a long time?

Use the same two cups—one of soil and one of water. Set them in a warm oven and leave them until they are almost the same temperature. Move them to a refrigerator and after ten minutes take the temperature of them. Take it again every ten minutes until you have discovered which cools off faster, land or water? Now you could figure out why in winter we may get warm breezes from off of a lake. It is because the water loses its heat more slowly than the land.

85

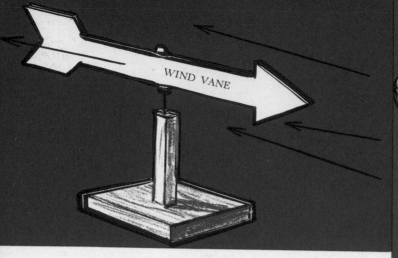

ANEMOMETER

WIND VANE

HOW CAN YOU MAKE A WIND VANE?

Cut two arrows out of heavy paper or tag board. Place a small glass bottle between the two arrows and then paste the arrows together. Put weight on the arrow until the paste is dry so that it will lie straight. Now make a support for the arrow. Your support could be a knitting needle standing up in a piece of wood, or a long nail. The bottle should turn freely on it. A wind vane is used to find the direction from which the wind is coming.

CAN YOU MAKE AN ANEMOMETER?

An anemometer is a wind gauge—it measures the speed of the wind. The one in the picture is made from a foil pie pan that frozen pies come in, 4 pieces of aluminum foil—6 inches square, and 4 strips of twisting tape or wire—9 inches long. Twist the tape or wire together into circles about 2½ inches in diameter. Fold the aluminum foil over the twisting tape into cup shapes. Staple or pin the cups firmly to the underside of the pie pan near the edge. The pan, you can use a paper plate, should then be mounted so it can turn freely.

The pan in the picture is mounted on a stick which has been set firmly in a plaster of Paris base. The plaster of Paris base is made by pouring plaster of Paris, which as been mixed with water into a thick paste, into a box and holding the stick in it until it begins to harden. Two metal circles which have been taken from the tops of tin cans help to hold the pie tin horizontal and to turn freely. You may wish to put the one you make on a fence where wind can reach it freely. The harder the wind blows the faster it will turn.

86

RAIN GAUGE

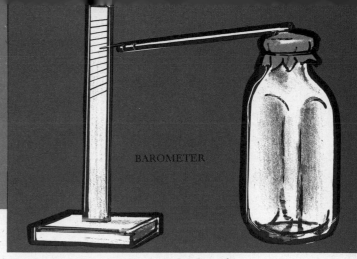

BAROMETER

CAN YOU MAKE A RAIN GAUGE?

Find a funnel and a glass jar. The top of the funnel should be the same size in diameter as the bottom of the jar. The bottom of the glass jar should be flat. Use a wax pencil and a ruler and mark each inch, half inch, and quarter inch on the outside of the jar. You will need to remember to make the measurements from the inside of the jar.

Set the glass jar in a coffee can and put sand around it so that it cannot tip over. Place the funnel in it securely—through a cork if one can be found which fits. Place the rain gauge in an open space so that rain can be caught in the funnel. Now the next time it rains you can see for yourself how big a rain it was.

CAN YOU MAKE A BAROMETER?

To make a barometer like the one in the picture all you need is a quart milk bottle, a piece of rubber, a straw and a needle.

Put the rubber over the mouth of the bottle stretched firmly but not tight. Hold it in place with a rubber band. Glue the straw to the rubber. Use Scotch tape and tape the pointer needle to the other end of the straw.

As the air pressure becomes greater on the outside than on the inside of the bottle it will push down harder on the rubber—then the needle will move up. When the air on the outside of the bottle has less pressure than the air on the inside the rubber will be pushed up. Then the needle will move down. This barometer does not tell what the air pressure is, but it shows whether the pressure is going up or down. Make a chart against which the movement of the needle can be seen.

87

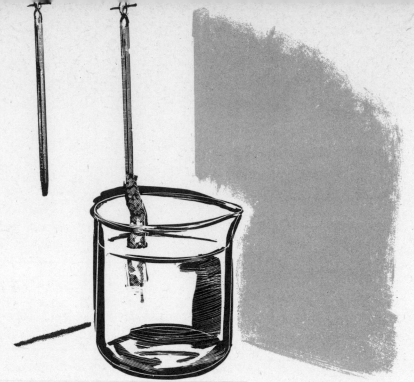

CAN YOU MAKE A HYGROMETER?

A hygrometer is an instrument which measures the amount of water (humidity) in the air. You will need two thermometers that are just alike. Use a piece of wick from an alcohol lamp. Slip one end of the wick over the bulb of one of the thermometers. Put the other end of the wick in a glass of water and put the two thermometers side by side against the wall. Some of the water from the glass will move up the wick and touch the bulb. Now read the thermometers. Fan both bulbs before you take a reading. There will be a difference. One thermometer takes the temperature of the air and the other has evaporating water around it. To understand how it works remember that evaporating water has a cooling effect. If you subtract the reading on one thermometer from that on the other you will have an idea of how much water there is in the air. If there is almost no difference you will know that there is a great deal of water in the air—that there was a great deal of water around the thermometer without the wick. If there are twelve or more degrees difference you will know that there is relatively little water in the air—not much water in the air around the thermometer with the wick.

You might be able to find a relative humidity chart which will give you the exact readings.

NOW
YOU
KNOW
THAT:

Meteorology is the study of weather.

Moisture in the air is called water vapor.

As warm air cools, water vapor collects in visible droplets.

When clouds become cool enough and heavy enough they drop their moisture as rain.

Frost is water vapor frozen into crystals of ice.

Snowflakes are arranged in sixes.

Air presses in all directions.

Warm air weighs less than the same amount of cold air.

Warm air rises as heavier cool air moves in.

A wind vane shows wind direction.

An anemometer measures wind speed.

A barometer measures air pressure.

A hygrometer measures moisture in the air.

89

LIGHT

On this page you see a picture of a striped scarf. Can you decide whether the black is on the white or the white on black? You will notice if you look at it one way it will look as though the black is on white, but if you look at it another way it will look as though the white is on black. If you look at the bottom of the page you will see a bit of the back of the scarf. Now you know that the black was on white. This is a trick our eyes play on us. It is an optical illusion.

92

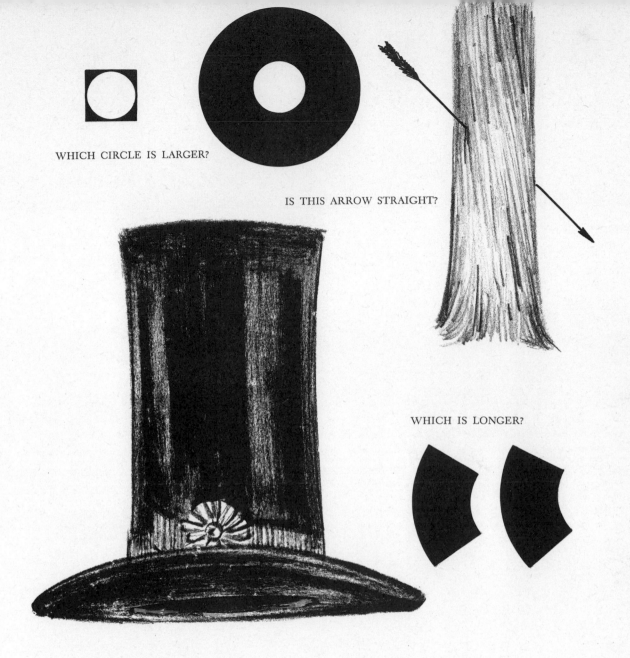

WHICH CIRCLE IS LARGER?

IS THIS ARROW STRAIGHT?

WHICH IS LONGER?

IS THE HAT TALLER THAN THE BRIM IS WIDE?

Look at the picture carefully and decide whether the hat is taller than the brim is wide. Now use a ruler and measure to find out for sure. You are probably surprised to find that they measure the same. This is an optical illusion.

Look at the other optical illusions pictured on this page. Can you answer the question? If you do some measuring you will know whether you answered the questions correctly.

Perhaps you can make some optical illusions for yourself.

93

DOES LIGHT TRAVEL IN A STRAIGHT LINE?

Use a card about four by six inches. Make a hole in the center
of the card about one-fourth inch in diameter. Light three candles
and place them in the room in three different places. Now look
through the hole of the card at one candle. Move the card as necessary
and find the other two candles one at a time. What was necessary
to see the candle? You probably discovered that you had to hold the
card so that the hole in it was exactly between the candle
and your eye. This is because light travels in a straight line.

94

HOW ARE WE ABLE TO SEE THINGS WHICH ARE NOT LIGHTED?

You will need to do this experiment at night. Use the same card which you used before. Turn on as many lights as you can in a room. Look at each of the lights through the hole in the card. Remember you can see the light because light travels in a straight line. Now pick an object which is not lighted and look at it through the card. Now turn the lights all off and look for the lights through the hole— of course you could not find them. The lights were not lighted. Now look for the unlighted object. Could you see it? You couldn't see it because it was not lighted. But it was not lighted before and you did see it. Can you explain? You are right if you say the light from the lighted lamp traveled in a straight line to the object. The object then reflected the light from its surface in a straight line to your eyes and you were able to see it. This explains how we see things which are not lighted.

95

HOW MANY DIMES CAN YOU GET FROM ONE DIME?

Use two mirrors at least three inches square. Lay the dime on a flat surface. Stand the mirrors so that they are side by side and the dime is in front of the edges of mirrors which touch. Now slowly move the outer edges of the mirrors inward. Be sure that the inner edges of the mirrors stay in place. How many dimes can you see? You are seeing reflections of reflections and may see several dimes.

HOW DO YOU READ A CLOCK WITH MIRRORS?

Stand an alarm clock with its back to you. Place a mirror in front of the clock. Now try to read the time. What do you notice? Now use two mirrors. Stand them with their two inner edges together. The clock should be facing the mirrors where they are touching each other. Now move the outer edges of the mirror toward you. Be sure to keep the inner edges touching each other. Now can you read the clock face? With one mirror, the reflection looked backwards to you. With two mirrors you discovered a reflection of a reflection and you could then read the clock.

A RULE FOR REFLECTED LIGHT

Stand three or more darning needles upright in a straight line about one-fourth inch apart across the end of a pad of white paper. Hold a lighted flashlight so that the light from the flashlight shines through between the needles and onto the pad of paper. There will be long dark shadows of the needles between the beams of light. Now stand a mirror upright diagonally across the shadows of needles and beams of light. You will see reflections of the shadows of the needles and of the beams of light. Do you notice that the reflected shadows and beams leave the mirror at the same angle at which they strike the mirror. This is a rule about light. Light is always reflected from a surface at the same angle at which it comes to it.

96

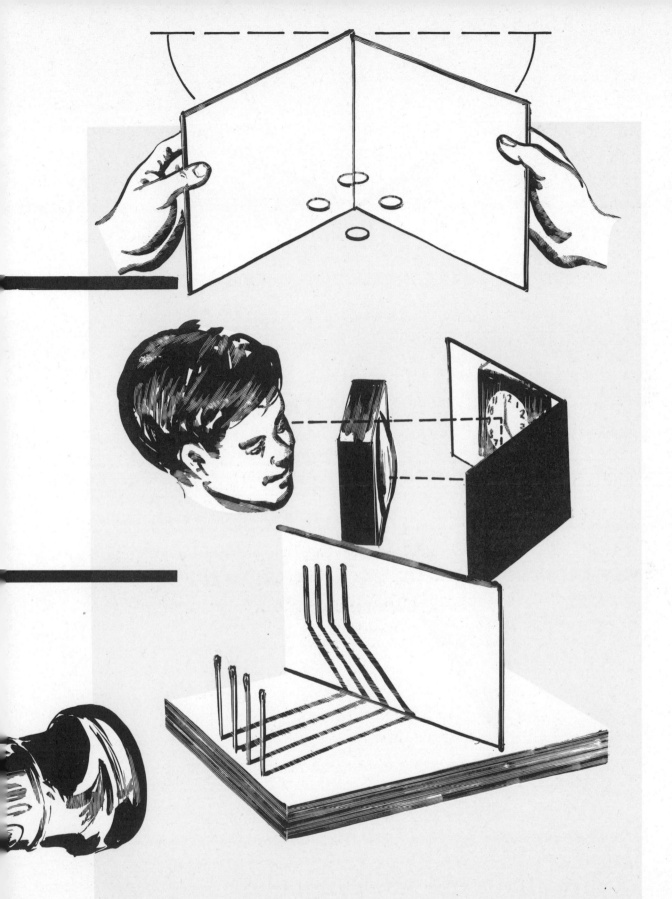

DOES THIS PENNY MOVE?

Place a penny in a pan. Arrange the penny and pan so that you can see only the edge of the penny which is farthest from you because the edge of the pan is in your way. Now ask a friend to pour water into the pan while you remain in the same position (don't move). What do you discover? You doubtless discovered that the penny appeared to move into your field of vision. But did the penny move—not really. The light rays changed their direction or path as they moved from the air into the water. They became bent and then you could see the penny. This is called refraction of light.

98

WHY DOES WATER MAGNIFY?

Fill a tall glass about three-fourths full of water. Place a kitchen knife blade end down into the water. Look at the blade above and below the water. You will discover that the blade looks bigger below the water level than above. This is because water magnifies. Water magnifies because the light rays are bent when they go from the air into the water.

HOW CAN YOU MAKE A MAGNIFYING LENS?

Use a piece of fine copper wire about six inches long. Wrap one end of the wire around a lead pencil and twist it so the wire makes a loop about one-fourth inch in diameter. Dip the loop in water. Look carefully and you will probably discover a thin film of water across the loop. If there is no film—dip it again. Now hold the wire so that the film of water is above printing in a book. You will notice that the printing is magnified when you look through the film of water. Water acts as a lens. This is a magnifying lens like the first one that man learned to use. These lenses may magnify as much as four or five times.

99

HOW CAN YOU SEE THE COLORS IN LIGHT?

Set a shallow pan of water in the sunshine. Place a small square
mirror upright in one end of the pan so that the sunshine strikes
the mirror both above and below the water level. Move it about slightly
until a band of rainbow colors appears somewhere on the wall.
Light is made up of all colors in the rainbow. This is called the spectrum.

100

OLD ROMAN
OIL LAMP

NOW
YOU
KNOW
THAT:

We see things which give off light
or which reflect light to our eyes.

You can see reflections of reflections.

We sometimes see optical illusions.

Light rays are bent as they move from
air into water. This is refraction.

Light travels in a straight line.

Lenses magnify because light rays
are bent or refracted.

Light rays are reflected from an
object at the same angle at which
they strike it.

Light is made up of all colors.

101

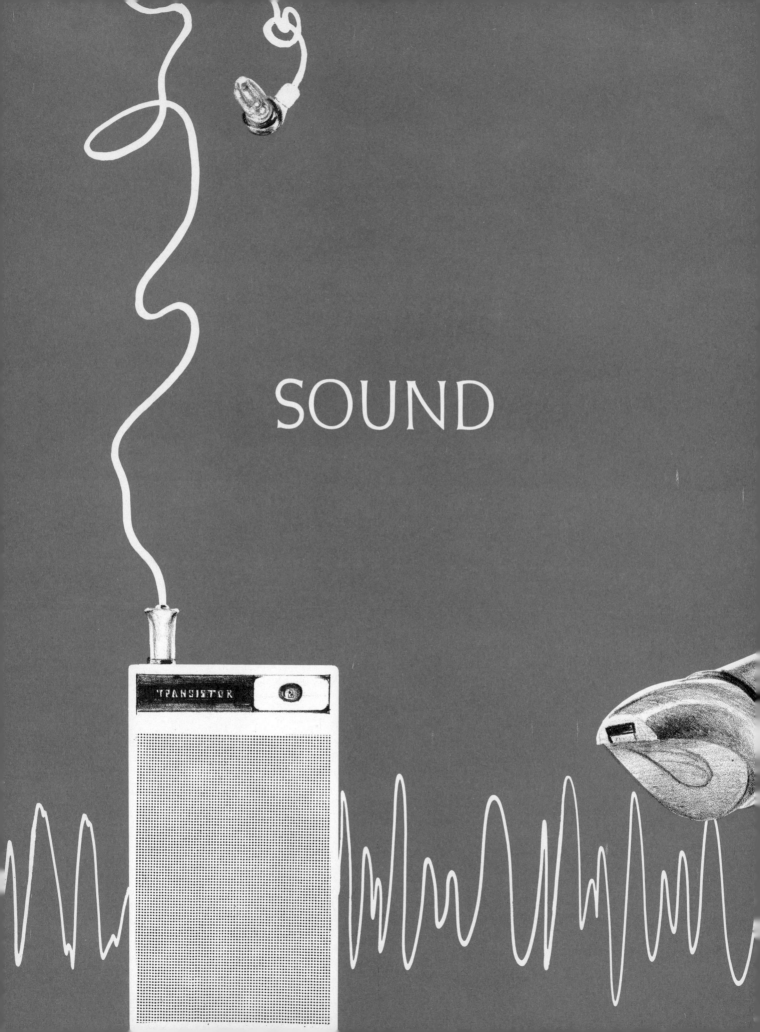

SOUND

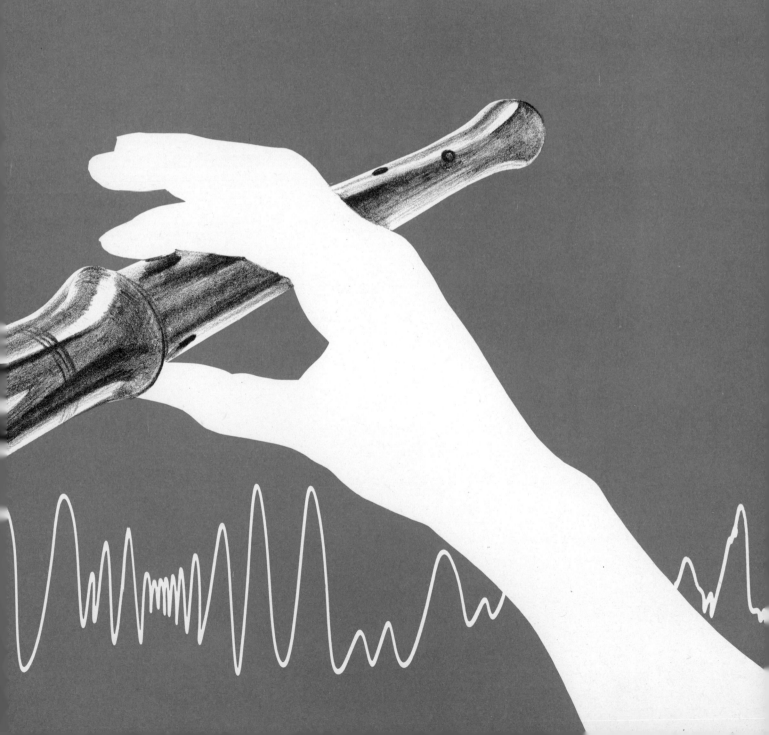

CAN YOU DISCOVER WHAT CAUSES SOUND?

Place your hand on your throat as the boy in the picture is doing.
Do you feel anything? Do you hear any thing? Now keep your
hand on your throat and say your name several times.
Do you feel any thing? You are sure to have heard your own voice.

Now loop a rubber band over something firm. Pull the other
end out with one hand. Can you hear anything? Now pluck it with your
other hand. Can you hear anything? Sound is caused by something
moving or vibrating. When you spoke your name your vocal cords
vibrated. When you plucked the rubber band it vibrated. You
have discovered for yourself what causes sound.

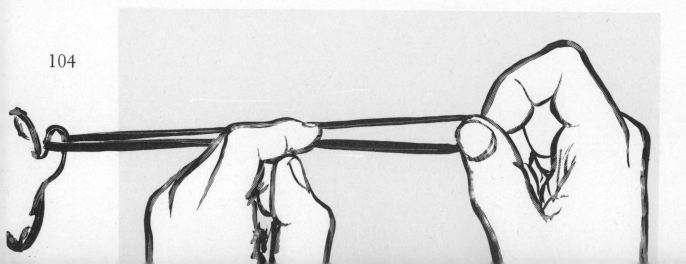

HOW CAN YOU SHOW THAT SOUND WAVES TRAVEL THROUGH AIR?

Light a candle. Put a tin can on its side with the open end of the
can about two inches from the lighted candle. The flame should
be near the center of the open end of the can. Hold the can firmly
and tap it hard on the bottom. Notice what happens to the flame
each time the bottom of the can is struck. The bottom of the can vibrates
and sets the air in the can to vibrating. The vibrating air causes
the flame to flicker or go out.

105

After discovering that sound is caused by vibration, you may wonder whether they are strong. Use a tuning fork. Hit one tine of the fork lightly on something solid. Now close your hand over the ends of the tines. Could you feel the vibrations? Fasten a ping pong ball to a string about 18 inches long, and fasten the other end of the string to something so the ball will swing freely. Strike one tine of the tuning fork and hold it to the ping pong ball (do not hit the ball). You probably will be surprised at the force with which the tuning fork sends the ball swinging.

106

Place an alarm clock on a table and set it ringing. Listen to it carefully. Now hold a solid metal rod so that one end of the rod rests on the clock and the other end is close to your ear. The sound will be louder through the metal rod because the solid metal carries sound better than air does.

Of course, you are sure to know that sounds can be made louder by making things vibrate farther. If you hit a tin can lightly— the sound is not very loud—hit it harder and the sound is louder. Hit the can very hard and the sound is very loud.

107

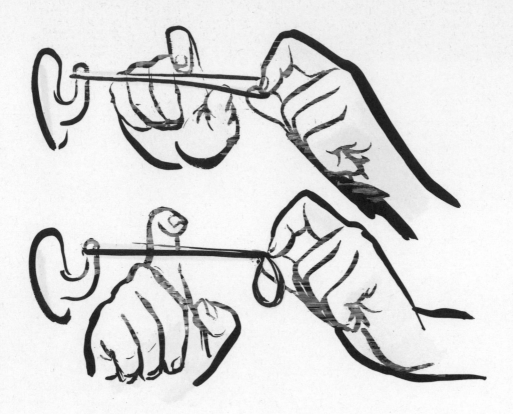

HOW CAN SOUNDS BE MADE HIGHER AND LOWER?

Now you know how sounds can be made louder. You probably wonder how they can be made higher or lower. You can discover something about this for yourself. Find a rubber band. Fasten one end of it securely to something firm. Stretch the band so that it is four inches long. Pluck it. Stretch it farther and hold it at a place four inches away from where it is fastened. Pluck it. Stretch it tighter and do the same thing. You will probably decide that the tighter the rubber band is stretched the higher the sound even though you hold it four inches away each time.

Find two rubber bands which are the same length but one heavier than the other. Fasten each of them securely and stretch each of them the same amount and pluck them. What did you discover? The thinner band produced the higher pitch, is probably your answer.

108   Pitch is dependent upon how many times a thing vibrates in a second. The length, thickness and tightness of a rubber band determines how many times it will vibrate in a second. This is not only true of rubber bands but of other things which make sound.

NOW
YOU
KNOW
THAT:

Sound is caused by something vibrating.

Sound waves travel better through some things than through others.

Pitch depends on the number of vibrations per second.

PEOPLE STUDY ABOUT MACHINES IN SCIENCE. THEY MAKE DISCOVERIES ABOUT HOW MACHINES CAN BE MADE TO DO WORK FOR US. A THING WHICH HELPS PUSH, PULL OR MOVE SOMETHING IS A MACHINE. WHEELS, LEVERS, AND INCLINED PLANES ARE THREE KINDS OF SIMPLE MACHINES. THE MORE COMPLICATED MACHINES HAVE SIMPLE MACHINES IN THEM.

SIMPLE MACHINES

Find an old broomstick. Saw about 4 inches off of the end of the handle. Now find a long narrow cardboard or wooden box. Measure the width of the box. If it is about 12 inches wide then saw another piece off of the broom handle, about 3 inches longer than the width of the box, or 15 inches. You will also need a piece of wood about 1 inch wide, ¼ inch thick and 6 inches long. A piece of good firm ruler would do. Tack the end of the piece of wood to the end of the long piece of broomstick and tack the end of the short piece of broom to the other end of the wood. It should look like this. You may need to use two tacks to keep it firmly together.

Now you are ready to put your machine together. Cut holes the size of the diameter of the broomstick in the sides of the box near the end of it. Stand the box on end and put the long piece of broomstick through the holes. Tack one end of a string to the broomstick near the center. Put a weight on the other end of the string. Turn the handle and see what happens. Your hand goes around in a circle and the string wraps around the stick—then the weight is lifted. You have found out how to make a windlass—a kind of machine. It can help you do work. The handle goes around in a circle like a wheel. The broomstick center of the wheel is the axle. The wheel seems to have only one spoke. A wheel is a simple machine.

112

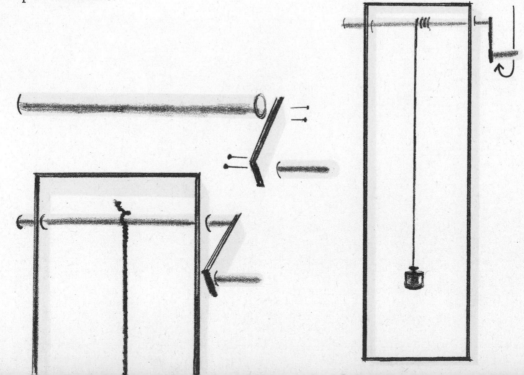

Fasten the wheels of your bicycle so that they cannot turn. Push the the bicycle along. Is it hard to push? Unfasten the wheels so that they roll. You will notice that wheels make it easier to move something.

Mark a place on the back wheel of your bicycle and mark a place on the ground. Stand the bicycle so that the marks are together. Move the bicycle until the wheel has turned around once. Measure the distance it moved. Measure the distance around the wheel. Were these two measurements almost the same? Set your bicycle up on its standard. Turn the pedals once. How many times did the front wheel turn around? How many times did the back wheel turn around? Did it turn around twice? Discover for yourself how far you can go with one turn of the pedals. This helps you to see how wheels make work easier for us. Wheels can be made to work together in many ways to give us speed and power. Wheels which work together in this way are called gear wheels.

113

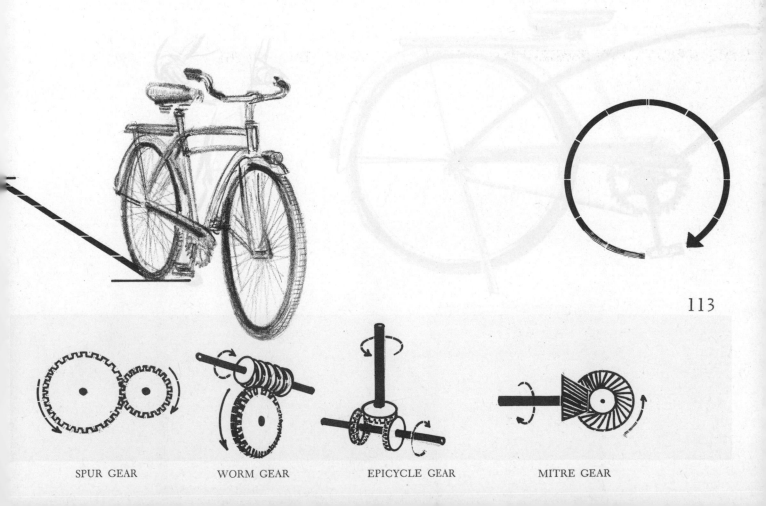

SPUR GEAR   WORM GEAR   EPICYCLE GEAR   MITRE GEAR

Find several file cards and cut six pieces each 3 inches long and 2½ inches wide from them. Fold one of the cards which you cut from one side to ¼ inch from the other side. Turn the card around and fold again in the same way. Now the card will have two folds ¼ inch apart. Fold each of the other cards in the same way. Paste the flat outside surfaces together and you will have a water wheel like this one.

Slide it onto a pencil and hold it under a stream of water. You will discover that the water pushing on the paddles of the wheel will cause it to turn around very fast. It is easy to see that if another wheel were fastened to the water wheel it would turn around fast, too. It could be made to work for us.

Water wheels can be made from wood. You might plan making one that will really do work for you.

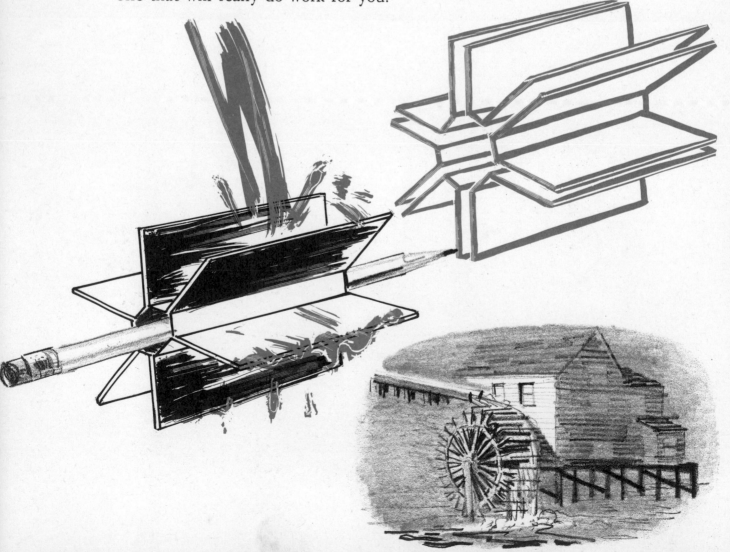

HOW CAN YOU PULL IN ONE DIRECTION AND MOVE SOMETHING IN
ANOTHER DIRECTION?

Find a board about 6 inches wide and 36 inches long. With a
sharp knife make a groove in the middle of an empty spool as you see
in the picture. Use a long nail and fasten the spool to one end of the
board, leaving enough space for the spool to turn freely. Now tie a
long string to a book, and place the string around the spool. Pull
down on the other end of the string—what happens—the book goes up
as you pull down. Now you know how a pulley may be used. It may be
used to pull in one direction and move a weight in the opposite direction.

Use the same board with the spool on it that you used in the experiment before this one. Find another empty spool and make a groove around the middle of it. Cut a piece of coat-hanger wire, put it through the spool and fasten the ends of the wire together. Be sure the spool can turn freely on the wire. Now fasten the book which you are about to lift to the loop of coat hanger wire. You are ready to put the string around your spool pulleys. Fasten one end of the string to the nail which holds the spool in place on the board, put the other end of the string around the groove of the spool which is fastened to the book. Now the string can be put in the groove on the other spool and allowed to hang down. Pull on the loose end of the string and see what happens. The book will probably be lifted. Is it harder or easier to lift the book with this pulley system than it was with the other experiment? It should be easier because you have more pulleys and string working for you.

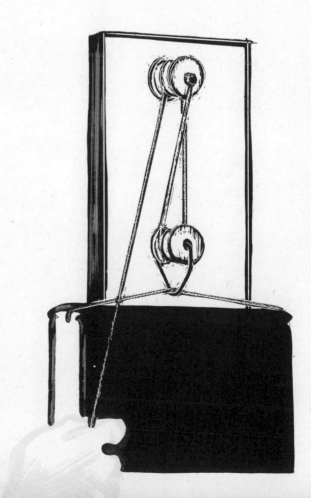

116

You might experiment with an inclined plane. Find a board about 6 inches wide and a toy truck. Put one end of the board on a brick and pull the toy truck up the board. Was it easy to do? Now put one brick on top of another and put one end of the board on them. Was it harder to pull the truck up now? It was harder but you pulled the truck up to a higher place. Now try the same thing with three and four bricks. Use a longer board. You will find that an inclined plane works for us. You move a thing a longer way, but it is easier than lifting it straight up.

HOW DO LEVERS HELP DO WORK?

This farmer found a big rock in his field and he wanted to move it. He could not lift it with his hands. He could lift it with the help of a pole. The pole was used as a lever. He put it under the rock and over a log and pushed down on it, and the rock came up.

Do some experiments with a lever like this one. Find a board about 30 inches long and 4 inches wide. Put a block of wood under the center of the board. Put a brick on one end of the board and push down on the other end. Did you need to push down hard? Now move the block of wood so that it is one-third the length or 10 inches from the end of the board. Place the brick as before. Now push down on the other end of the board. You probably noticed that it was easier but that your hand had to move farther, but the brick did not go so far. Now move the block of wood two-thirds the length or 20 inches from the end where the brick is. You will notice that you push harder, your hand does not go so far, but the brick moves farther.

Try this same experiment with the brick in different positions. You will discover that the closer the block of wood is to the brick the easier it is to lift, but also your hand will need to move farther.

118

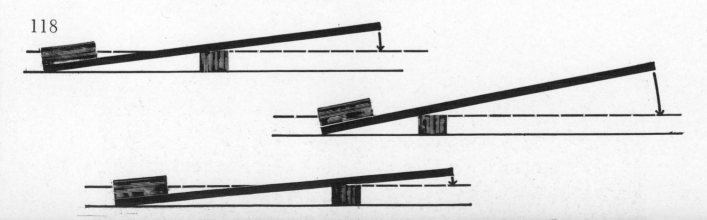

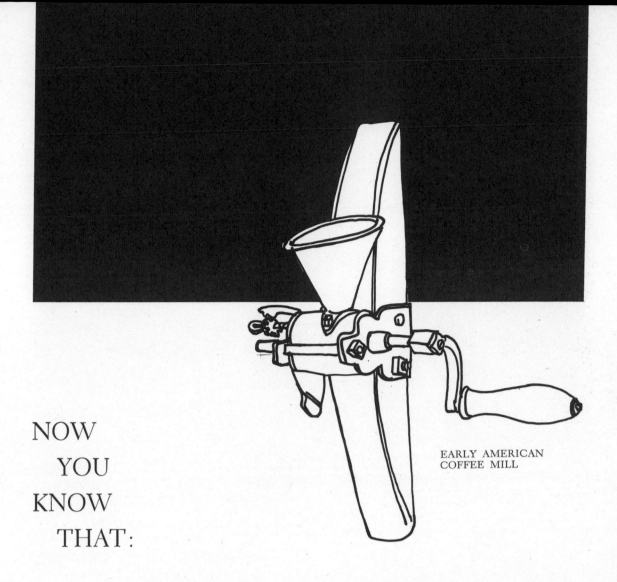

EARLY AMERICAN
COFFEE MILL

NOW
YOU
KNOW
THAT:

Wheels, levers and inclined planes are three kinds of simple machines.

We use wheels and levers to do work for us in many ways.

Complicated machines have simple machines in them.

Wheels; levers and inclined planes help us to make work easier.

LIVING

BIOLOGY IS THE STUDY OF LIVING THINGS. LIVING THINGS ARE EITHER PLANTS OR ANIMALS. SCIENTISTS WHO STUDY PLANTS ARE KNOWN AS BOTANISTS. SCIENTISTS WHO STUDY ANIMALS ARE KNOWN AS ZOOLOGISTS. BOTH BOTANISTS AND ZOOLOGISTS ARE DISCOVERING NEW THINGS ABOUT PLANTS AND ANIMALS EVERY DAY.

THINGS

WHAT ARE LIVING THINGS?

On this page are pictures of things which are alive and of things which are not alive. Which of them are pictures of living things and which are not? These hints will help you.

Livings things grow.

Living things produce living things like themselves.

Living things need air, food and water.

Of course you know that the hamster, bean plant, kitten and little girl are pictures of living things. Did you put the snowball with them? It does grow bigger but not in the way living things grow. It grows bigger when layers of snow are added to the outside of it. Living things grow bigger from the inside. They need food, air and water.

122

On this page are pictures of twelve animals. If you were asked to divide them into two groups how would you do it? You might say some fly and some do not. Some swim and some do not. Some live in water and others on land. Any of these ways would be good ways. You can discover another way if you will find out about the skeletons or bones of these animals. You will discover that some of these animals have backbones but other animals do not have backbones— in fact they have no bones. Your two groups would be like this:

With backbones		*Without backbones*
Bat	Robin	Grasshopper
Whale	Turtle	Monarch butterfly
Goldfish		Spider
Frog		Snail
Pony		Earthworm

123

Here are pictures of twelve animals which have backbones. They are different in other ways though. They can be grouped or classified into five groups. To group them it is important to know certain things about them.

Do they have feathers?

Do they have fur or hair?

Do they have fins?

Do they have scales and lungs?

Do they have gills and later in their life lungs?

Now try classifying the animals. Your classification should be something like this:

Feathers	Hair or fur	Fins	Scales and lungs	Lungs and gills
Robin	Beaver	Trout	Snake	Toad
Bluebird	Raccoon	Seahorse	Turtle	Frog
	Dog			Newt

Think of names of other animals with backbones. Can you find a place in one of the groups for each of them? This is one way that animals with backbones are classified.

Mammals have fur or hair.

Birds have feathers.

Reptiles have scales and lungs.

Amphibians have gills and later get lungs.

Fish have fins.

124

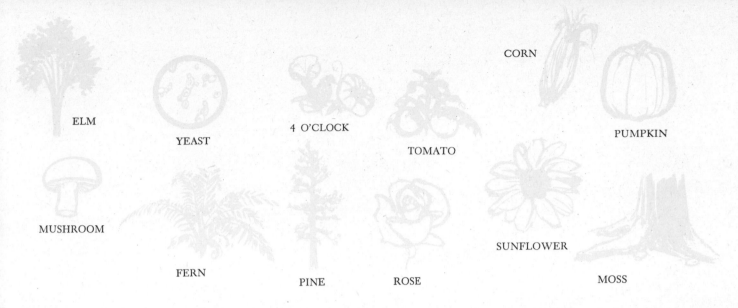

ELM

YEAST

4 O'CLOCK

CORN

TOMATO

PUMPKIN

MUSHROOM

FERN

PINE

ROSE

SUNFLOWER

MOSS

HOW CAN PLANTS BE DIVIDED INTO TWO GROUPS?

There are pictures of twelve plants on this page. See if you can find a way to divide them into two groups. Remember they may not always look just as they do in the pictures. You may try dividing them according to color of flower but you will find that does not work. Not all of them have flowers. You might try dividing them into those with woody stems and those without. This is a good way to do it. You may discover for yourself another good way—those which are green and those which are not green. If you did this you would have the yeast and mushroom in one group and all the others in another group. Here is another plan which you may have discovered for yourself. Those which produce and those that do not produce seeds. If you divide them this way you will have two lists such as this:

With seeds	*Without seeds*
Elm tree	Yeast plant
Pumpkin	Fern
Pine tree	Moss
Rose	Mushroom
Sunflower	
Tomato	
Corn	
Four-o'clock	

Scientists use all of these ways. This is the way they classify plants.

125

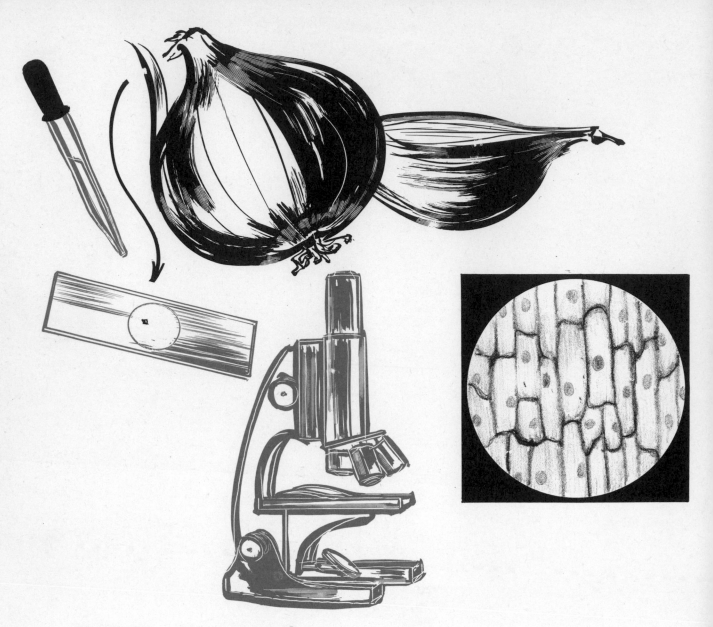

WHAT ARE ONIONS MADE OF?

You can do this experiment if you have a microscope. Cut an onion in half. You will notice that the onion bulb is made up of layers. Remove one of these layers. On the outside of it you will find a very thin skin of tissue. Peel off a bit of it and place it on your microscope slide. Drop a drop of water on it and cover it with one of the cover glasses. Now you are ready to look at your slide through the microscope.

126

You will discover that the onion is made up of cells much like those you see in the picture. All living things are made of cells but not all cells look alike.

WHO LIVES HERE?

Measure off a square yard in a partly grassy place in a woods. Examine the area carefully and make a notation or drawing on a card of every kind of living thing you see. Include those which walk, crawl, or fly over it as well as those you find coming out of the ground. Dig into the ground a bit in several spots to see whether you can find more to add to your list.

Now separate your notation cards into two piles—plants and animals. Were you surprised at the number which you found?

SPANISH
NEEDLE

MAPLE SEED

TUMBLEWEED

BUTTERPRINT

HOW DO SEEDS GET SCATTERED?

On this page are pictures of eight kinds of plants with seeds. Three words suggest ways in which seeds get carried from one place to another—wind, water, animals.

OAT

Can you decide which one helps scatter the seeds in the pictures? You probably decided that wind helps elm, tumbleweed, and butterprint to get scattered. Oats will float on water and animals carry the rest. These decisions are good ones.

Look at each of the seeds and see what it has which helps wind, water or animals carry it. You will notice hooks or spines which catch onto animal fur or onto clothing. The walnuts and pumpkin seeds are carried about because they make good food. Some, such as oats, have air spaces and float. The elm has wings and the tumbleweed rolls about in the wind. Wind helps butterprint to scatter its seeds because the seed pod is like a shaker, when the wind blows. Find other seeds and see whether they get carried in any of these ways.

PUMPKIN
SEED

HOW DO NUMBERS OF SEEDS COMPARE?

Get a peach, an apple, and a canteloupe. Cut each of them open and count all the seeds you find in each of them. You might try this over again and see whether you found the same numbers. The numbers probably were not exactly the same. Each time there were a few more apple seeds than peach seeds and many more canteloupe seeds than apple seeds. You were probably very much surprised at the number of seeds you found in the canteloupe. Can you think of any good ideas about ways in which it might be helpful for some fruits to have so many seeds? One idea might be that there are not so many canteloupes as there are peaches or apples. Another idea would be that many more of some kinds of seeds get destroyed and never have a chance to grow.

128

Remove the seed from a fresh avocado. Find three toothpicks
and push the ends of each of them into the side of the seed. They should
be arranged as they are in the picture on this page. Fill a glass with water.
Place the seed with the point up over the top of the glass. The toothpicks
will keep it from falling into the glass. The lower part of the seed will
be in the water. You will need to add water almost every day. It may
take some time for the seed to start to grow. If one seed does not grow
then start another. As it grows it will look like this

and this.

129

WHAT DO YEAST PLANTS LOOK LIKE?

Fill a cup about half full of slightly warm water. In the water put 1 teaspoonful of sugar and ¼ teaspoonful of powdered dry yeast. Let this stand for an hour. Place a drop of this yeast solution on a slide and cover it with a cover slip. Look at this through a microscope. Can you see many cells that look much like those in the picture? Those cells are yeast plants.

130

HOW DOES YEAST MAKE BREAD RISE?

Get two bowls of exactly the same size. Into each of them put ½ cup of slightly warm water. Add 1 teaspoonful of sugar to each of them. To one of them add about ¼ teaspoonful of powdered dry yeast. Now to each of them add ½ cup of flour, and mix thoroughly. Set both bowls aside in a moderately warm place. At the end of an hour examine both of them. Do you see a difference? Can you taste a difference? Can you explain why there are so many bubbles in one of them but not in the other? Remember one of the bowls had no yeast in it—otherwise they were alike. This shows clearly that it must be yeast which causes the bubbles.

Yeast uses sugar as its food. Carbon dioxide and alcohol are given off as the yeast grows and develops new plants. The bubbles are bubbles of carbon dioxide.

This experiment gives you an idea of how bread is made. If you add another half cup of flour to each bowl and mix the contents of each of them into a soft dough you have in one of them the kind of dough from which bread is baked. Let both of these bowls of dough set for a couple more hours and then look at them. Can you explain why one is so much bigger than the other? It is because of the carbon dioxide bubbles in the dough. If the bread is baked the gas escapes and the bread is full of air spaces. You might wish to bake both of the little loaves of dough and see the difference.

131

BLACK BREAD-MOLD

CAN YOU MAKE A MOLD GARDEN?

Select an orange, a slice of moist bread, and a spoonful of jelly. Put all these foods on a plate and cover them with a glass jar—this is your mold garden. Set this garden in a warm dark place. Examine your garden each day. Soon you will see mold of different colors appear on the foods. There will probably be a black-colored mold on the bread. There might be a blue-green mold on the orange, as well as on the jelly. There are many different kinds and colors of molds and they grow on different kinds of things.

If you have a microscope you might put a bit of mold from the bread on a glass slide and cover it with a cover glass. Your mold may look like this black mold in the picture.

132

NOW
YOU
KNOW
THAT:

AFTER LEONARDO'S PROPORTIONS
OF THE HUMAN FIGURE, 1492

Biology is the study of all living things. Botanists study plants. Zoologists study animals.

Living things grow from the inside.

Living things need food, air and water.

Living things produce living things like themselves.

There are different ways of grouping plants and animals.

Living things are usually grouped on the basis of their structure.

All living things are made of cells.

Wind, water, animals help scatter seeds.

133

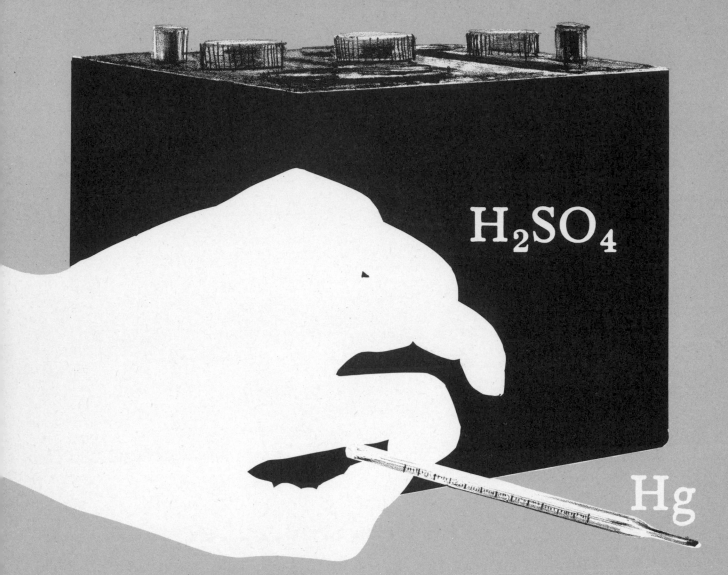

H_2SO_4

Hg

WHAT THINGS ARE

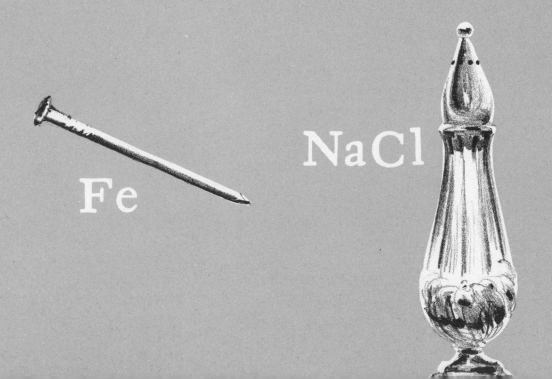

Fe

NaCl

CHEMISTRY IS THE STUDY OF WHAT THINGS ARE MADE OF AND THE CHANGES THEY UNDERGO. A SCIENTIST WHO WORKS IN THE FIELD OF CHEMISTRY IS CALLED A CHEMIST.

IF YOU VISIT A CHEMIST'S LABORATORY YOU WILL PROBABLY SEE MANY BOTTLES PROPERLY LABELED. THEY MIGHT HAVE SUCH LABELS AS NaCl, Fe, Hg, H_2SO_4, $C_{12}H_{22}O_{11}$, AND Cu ON THEM. YOU CAN FIND OUT THE COMMON NAMES OF THE CONTENTS OF THESE BOTTLES IF YOU LOOK AT THE PICTURES ON THIS PAGE. TO UNDERSTAND WHAT THE SYMBOLS MEAN YOU NEED TO KNOW THAT SCIENTISTS BELIEVE ALL THINGS TO BE MADE OF MOLECULES, AND THAT THE MOLECULES ARE MADE OF ONE OR MORE ATOMS. THE ATOMS MAY BE ALL ALIKE OR THEY MAY BE DIFFERENT. THE Fe MEANS IRON AND IT SHOWS THAT THERE IS NOTHING BUT IRON ATOMS IN IT. IN EACH SALT MOLECULE THERE IS ONE ATOM OF SODIUM AND ONE ATOM OF CHLORINE. SUGAR MOLECULES HAVE SEVERAL ATOMS OF THREE DIFFERENT ELEMENTS IN EACH MOLECULE. THERE ARE MORE THAN A HUNDRED KNOWN ELEMENTS AND ALL THINGS ARE MADE UP OF THESE OR DIFFERENT COMBINATIONS OF THESE ELEMENTS. IF YOU HAVE A CHEMISTRY SET YOU MAY DISCOVER THAT THE CHEMICALS IN IT ARE LABELED WITH SYMBOLS TOO.

MADE OF

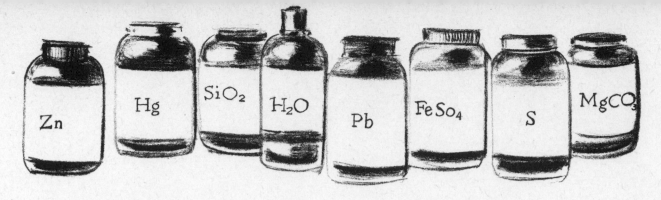

ARE THESE BOTTLES FILLED WITH ELEMENTS OR COMPOUNDS?

On this page are pictures of eight different bottles. Four of them have compounds in them. A compound is made up of molecules that have more than one kind of element in them. For example, water is a compound because it is made up of Hydrogen and Oxygen (H_2O). See whether you can decide by the symbols which are elements and which are compounds. Did you decide that the symbols written with only a capital letter or a capital letter and little letter were symbols of elements? This is true. The Hg, Pb, S and the Zn were all elements. The rest were compounds. You could discover what elements are in the compounds by looking at the list of symbols at the end of this section.

ARE THINGS EITHER ELEMENTS OR COMPOUNDS?

Fill a cup with sand. Fill another cup with salt. Now pour the sand into a bowl and pour the salt on top of it. Mix them thoroughly. Examine what you have. Can you find a grain of sand? Can you find a grain of salt? You have a mixture of salt and sand. This is not a compound because there are molecules of both salt and sand in it—it is therefore a mixture. The air which we breathe is a mixture of the molecules of several gases of which it is made.

136

Get one ice cube from a refrigerator. Put it in a small beaker. Put an alcohol lamp under the beaker and watch the ice cube. You are sure to know what will happen—it will melt.

But notice too that almost immediately some steam comes from inside the beaker. As soon as melting begins, water begins evaporating. Soon the ice cube will be completely melted. Keep on watching—the water begins to boil. Do you see the steam going off into the air? Before long all the water is gone into the air. You have seen water when it is a solid, a liquid and a gas. When it was a solid it had a shape of its own and the molecules were close together. When the water was a liquid it was the shape of the container which held it and the molecules were farther apart than when it was a solid. When the water went off into the air the molecules moved very far apart and were mixed with the molecules of the other gases in the air.

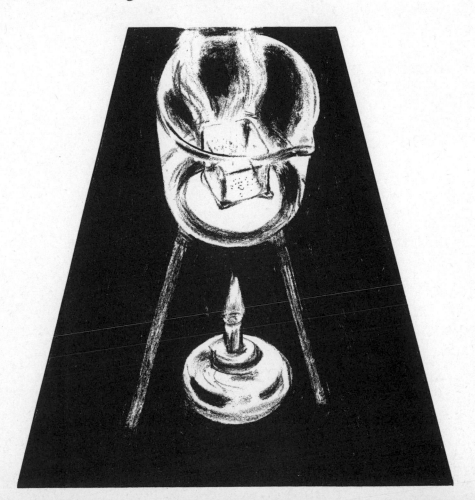

HOW CAN THESE THINGS BE GROUPED?

Find three bottles which are all about the same size. Put a cork in one of them. Fill one with water and put a cork in it. Fill the third one with sand and put a cork in it. One has air, one has water, and one has sand but there is another way in which these things are different. Look at this list of things and see whether you can divide them so that part of them would belong with the air bottle, some with the water bottle, and the rest of them with the sand—water vapor, ice, sugar, oxygen, pencil, milk, mercury, ink, erasure, carbon dioxide, pin, syrup, nail. When you have them grouped can you give a name to each group? Here is the way of grouping which you probably decided to use.

Gases	Liquids	Solids	
Air	Water	Sand	Pin
Water vapor	Milk	Ice	Nail
Oxygen	Mercury	Sugar	
Carbon Dioxide	Ink	Pencil	
	Syrup	Erasure	

   Get a glass of cold, clear water. Drop two drops of red food coloring into it. Do not stir it. Watch what happens. Do you see pink clouds floating here and there in the clear water? After one-half hour look at it again. Let it set over night. What do you notice in the morning? The water will be tinted all through it in the morning. The colored liquid will be distributed evenly throughout the water. In other words, the molecules of food coloring and molecules of water are all mixed together. This is called diffusion.

HOW CAN SOME SOLIDS BE MADE INTO LIQUIDS?

Everyone knows that if ice is left in a temperature which is above freezing that it will melt. There are other ways in which solids may be made into liquids. Fill a cup with warm water. Stir into it a teaspoonful of sugar. Did the sugar melt? We say that the sugar dissolved. The molecules of sugar mixed up with the molecules of water and we could no longer see the sugar. We have a sugar solution. Add another teaspoonful of sugar. Did it dissolve? Now we have a stronger sugar solution. Continue to add sugar until no more will dissolve. Now you have a saturated solution. Many things can be made into liquids by dissolving them in water.

Fill two cups, which are exactly alike, with water. The water in one of them should be very cold and the water in the other should be very hot. Add a teaspoonful of salt to each of them at the same time. Which of them dissolved the faster? Add another teaspoonful of salt to each of them at the same time and see which dissolves the faster. You may need to repeat this experiment several times to be sure of your answer. You probably discovered that the salt in the hot water dissolved faster. Molecules move faster in hot water than in cold water therefore the salt dissolves faster.

141

WILL EVERYTHING DISSOLVE IN WATER?

For this experiment you will need two beakers which are exactly the same size, two crystals of camphor gum and alcohol. The kind you use in an alcohol lamp will do. Put water in one beaker and alcohol in the other so that they are filled to the same height. Now drop the crystals of camphor gum into the two beakers at exactly the same time. Watch them carefully. What happens to the one in the alcohol? What happens to the one in water? Try this over again. Did the same thing happen? You may need to do it several times to be sure of your answer. You are correct if you decide that water does not dissolve camphor gum, but alcohol does dissolve camphor gum. No, not everything dissolves in water.

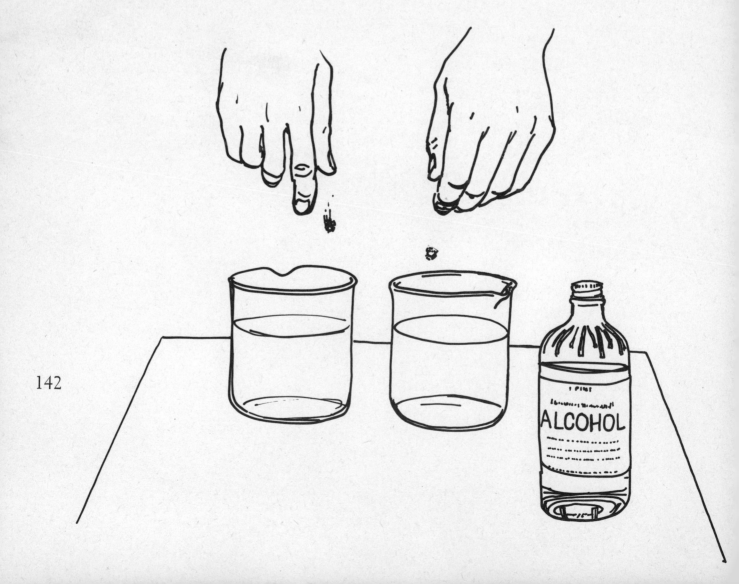

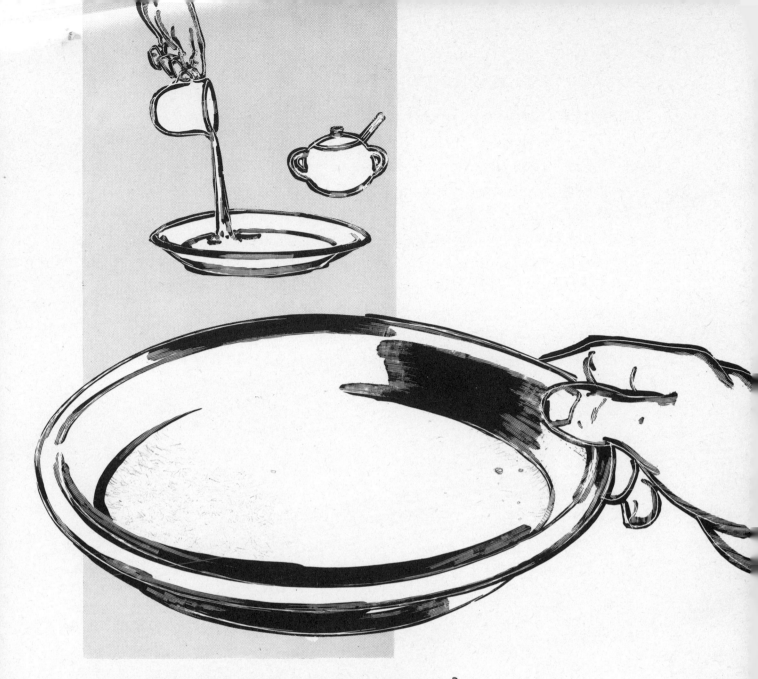

HOW CAN WE GET SUGAR OUT OF A SUGAR SOLUTION?

Stir about three tablespoonfuls of sugar into one-half cup of water. Stir
until all of the sugar has been dissolved. Now pour the sugar
solution into a pie tin and set it aside. Check it every few hours to
see what is happening to it. After a period of time the water will
have evaporated and the sugar will be left in the pan. The sugar may
not look exactly as it did before it was dissolved but it is still sugar—it
is made of the same elements as it was before. It has
gone through a physical change.

143

WHAT HAPPENS TO SUGAR WHEN IT IS HEATED?

Put a tablespoonful of sugar in a pan and set it on the stove. Keep the heat low at first. What do you see happening to the sugar? Perhaps you think it is melting. It does begin to melt, then it begins to change color, turns brown. It will soon begin to burn and after a few minutes the sugar will be burned leaving only a spot of black carbon. You have produced a chemical change. You have no sugar—there is only carbon left. The hydrogen and oxygen that was in the sugar have gone off into the air. Some of the hydrogen and oxygen combined and formed water and then disappeared into the air.

HOW DOES HARD WATER ACT WITH SOAP IN IT?

Fill two glasses about ½ full of water from the faucet. To one of
them add one teaspoonful of Epsom salts. This will make the water
in the glass very hard. Dissolve some soap in a cup of water. Now add
one half of the cup of soapy water to one glass of water and
the other half to the other glass of water with Epsom salts in it. Stir each
of them. You will notice that the water in one glass becomes thick
with soap suds. The other glass—the one in which the water
has been made especially hard with Epsom salts—has almost no suds
in it. Instead there is a sticky white scum. The hard minerals
in the water combined with the soap and made it
useless—it could not do its work.

145

Fill a flask about ½ full of water from the faucet. The water from the faucet is hard—that is it has some minerals dissolved in it but you might add a teaspoonful of Epsom salts to it to be sure it is very hard water. Now put a cork with a glass tube through it in the flask. A rubber tube on the other end of the glass tube should lead into a test tube or small beaker. Light an alcohol lamp and put it under the flask. Soon the water will begin to boil. The steam will fill the top of the flask and go through the glass tube and rubber tube and into the test tube or small beaker. As soon as the steam cools it turns back to water. Water will collect in the test tube or beaker. It is very soft water—distilled water. It will have no minerals in it. The minerals are all left behind in the boiling water.

You might like to do this same experiment and put some red food coloring in the flask. Would you expect the distilled water to be red, too? You are correct if you predict that it won't be red.

146

WHAT IS SNOW MADE OF?

You think that you know the answer to this question. The answer
is water—but you might discover that snow is made of something
other than water. If you try this experiment you will need a glass and
some snow. Fill the glass with snow so that there is no space left
at the top. Do not pack it in. Set the glass aside for an hour. Now
examine the glass. Is it full of water? Remember it was full of snow. It
is now full of water and air. In fact, there is more air than water.
This was true of the snow too. Snowflakes are made of crystals
of ice and air—more air than ice crystals.

NOW
YOU
KNOW
THAT:

Chemistry is the study of what things are made of and changes they may undergo.

There are about 100 known elements.

All things are made of molecules of these elements or of molecules which are combinations of them.

A chemical symbol shows the make-up of a molecule of a substance.

Things may be classified as gases, liquids or solids.

Not all things dissolve in water.

Warm water dissolves things faster than cold water.

Anything which goes through a physical change is made of the same elements as before.

Anything which goes through a chemical change has been changed so that it is not made of the same elements as before.

Snowflakes are made of ice crystals and air.

148

ANCIENT CHEMICAL SYMBOLS

LIST OF SYMBOLS FOR SOME OF THE ELEMENTS
A full table of elements can be found in a dictionary.

Symbol	Element	Description
Al	Aluminum	Light-weight, silvery metal
A	Argon	Colorless gas
B	Boron	Yellow or brown solid
Ca	Calcium	Soft, silvery metal
C	Carbon	Clear crystals or black solid
Cl	Chlorine	Heavy, greenish-yellow gas
Cr	Chromium	Hard, grayish-white metal
Co	Cobalt	Gray metal
Cu	Copper	Reddish metal
Au	Gold	Yellow metal
He	Helium	Colorless gas
H	Hydrogen	Colorless gas
I	Iodine	Dark, crystalline solid
Fe	Iron	Silver-white metal
Pb	Lead	Heavy, gray metal
Mg	Magnesium	Gray metal
Mn	Manganese	Dull, reddish metal
Hg	Mercury	Heavy, silvery liquid
Ne	Neon	Colorless gas
Ni	Nickel	Gray metal
N	Nitrogen	Colorless gas
O	Oxygen	Colorless gas
P	Phosphorus	Waxy, white solid
Pt	Platinum	Silvery metal
K	Potassium	Blue-white metal
Si	Silicon	Gray crystals
Ag	Silver	White metal
Na	Sodium	Gray metal
S	Sulphur	Yellow solid
Sn	Tin	Silvery metal
W	Tungsten	Silvery metal
Zn	Zinc	Blue-gray metal

MORE

THINGS TO DO

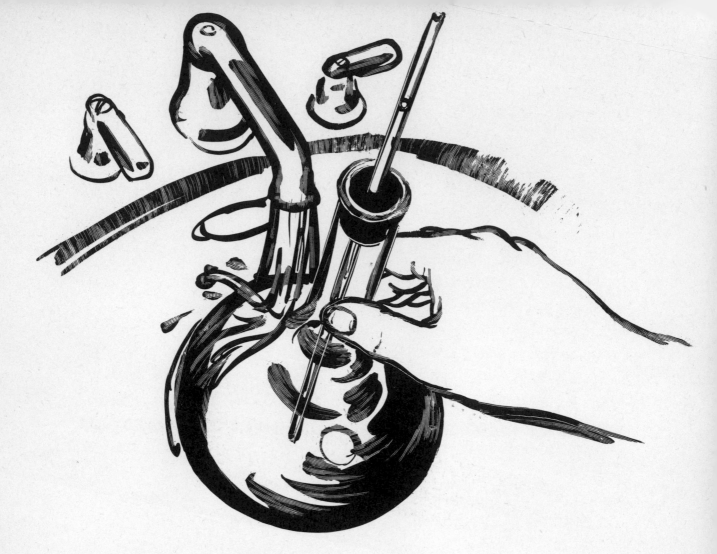

WHAT HAPPENS TO WATER WHEN IT IS HEATED?

Fill a flask full of water from the cold water faucet. Put a cork with a glass tube through it into the neck of the flask. You will notice that water is forced up into the tube as you put the cork in place. Mark the height of the water with a piece of string or a wax pencil. Now hold the flask so that hot water from the faucet runs down over it. Soon you will see something happening—the water moving up in the tube. Water expands as it is heated and takes up more room. When it expands the molecules in it move faster and farther apart.

Now allow the water to cool and see what happens. You may wish to set the flask in a very cool place and see whether the water level will go below the marked place on the tube. The next experiment will show you why you should not put your flask in a place where the water in it will freeze.

152

Find a jar with a screw-top lid.
Fill the jar completely full of water and screw the lid on tight. Now
wrap the jar in a cloth and put it in the freezer section of your
refrigerator, or put it outdoors if the temperature is well below freezing.
Leave it over night or for several hours. When you examine it you
will be almost sure to find the jar broken. You are probably very
much puzzled over this discovery if you remember that in another
experiment you discovered that water expanded as it was heated and
contracted as it cooled. Water does contract as it is cooled
to a certain temperature, then it begins to expand.
It was the expansion that broke your jar. Water is unusual in this respect.

DOES AIR ALWAYS TRAVEL IN A STRAIGHT LINE?

Stand a round milk bottle in front of a lighted candle. The candle
should be about one-third as tall as the milk bottle is and it should
be standing about two inches from the bottle. Now blow directly
on the bottle. What happened? Did the candle go out? Did you blow
through the bottle? The air actually goes around the bottle
and comes together at the point near the flame causing it to go out
or to almost go out. From this you can see that air does
not always travel in a straight line.

153

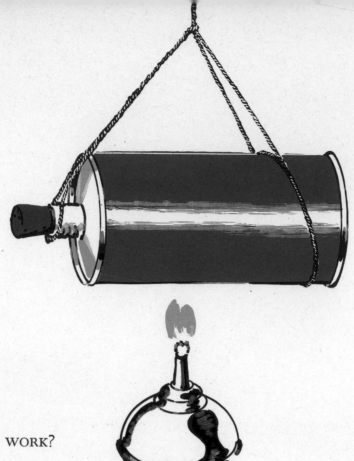

CAN GAS DO WORK?

Find an empty tin detergent can. Rinse it out so that it is very clean. Put one teaspoonful of alcohol in the can and put a rubber stopper in the opening to the can. Now make a swing out of string as you see in the picture and fasten the end of the string to a rod. Place an alcohol lamp under the can and light the lamp. The can should not be in the flame but about two inches above it.

You probably already know that alcohol evaporates very quickly and even more quickly when it is heated. It, of course, becomes a gas as it evaporates. From this idea you can predict what will probably happen. The gas inside the can will exert pressure. Finally the pressure will be great enough to force the cork out of the can. If you watch carefully you will see the can swing backwards as the cork comes out. It goes backwards because the cork and gas (evaporated alcohol and air) coming out push against the air on the outside. If we had taken the cork out of the can and made the can to swing we would have been doing some work. This way the gas did work for us. If you do this experiment be sure to use a tin can— a glass bottle might break.

154

NOW
YOU
KNOW
THAT:

Water expands when heated.

Water contracts as it cools to a certain point, then it expands as it freezes.

Expanding gas can be made to work for us.

INDEX

Suggested sources where science materials
can be obtained

HOME
Aluminum foil
Balls
Candles
Clay
Coffee can
Coal
Cups, tin, paper
Darning needles
Electric fan
Epsom salts
Food coloring
Grass seed
Knitting needles
Nails
Pans, foil, tin

HARDWARE STORE
Aluminum foil
Bulbs, small light
Copper wire
Dry cell
Flashlight
Flashlight battery
Rods, brass, wooden
Sockets, electric
Switches, electric
Thermometers

DRUGSTORE
Alcohol
Alum, powdered
Balloons
Blotting paper
Camphor gum
Candles
Clay
Corks
Epsom salts
File cards
Flashlight battery
Iodine
Limewater
Paper cups
Plaster of Paris
Straws

CHEMISTRY SET or
SCIENCE KIT
Alcohol
Alcohol lamp
Beakers
Corks
Flasks
Funnels
Iron filings
Magnets
Microscope
Stoppers, rubber
Thermometers
Tuning fork

157